ALSO BY CHUCK BARRIS

Who Killed Art Deco?

The Big Question

Confessions of a Dangerous Mind

Bad Grass Never Dies: The Sequel to "Confessions of a Dangerous Mind"

The Game Show King

You and Me, Babe: A Novel

DELLA

A Memoir of My Daughter

CHUCK BARRIS

Simon & Schuster
New York London Toronto Sydney

Simon & Schuster
1230 Avenue of the Americas
New York, NY 10020

First Simon & Schuster hardcover edition June 2010

SIMON & SCHUSTER and colophon are registered trademarks
of Simon & Schuster, Inc.

For information about special discounts for bulk purchases,
please contact Simon & Schuster Special Sales at
1-866-506-1949 or business@simonandschuster.com.

The Simon & Schuster Speakers Bureau can bring authors
to your live event. For more information or to book an event,
contact the Simon & Schuster Speakers Bureau at
1-866-248-3049 or visit our website at www.simonspeakers.com.

Designed by Jill Putorti

Manufactured in the United States of America

10   9   8   7   6   5   4   3   2   1

Library of Congress Cataloging-in-Publication Data
Barris, Chuck.
Della: a memoir of my daughter / Chuck Barris.
    p. cm.
1. Barris, Chuck. 2. Television producers and directors—United States—Biography.
3. Authors, American—20th century—Biography. 4. Barris, Della, 1962–1998.
5. Fathers and daughters—United States—Biography. I. Title.
PN1992.4.B37A3   2010
791.4502'80922—dc22   2009048675
[B]

ISBN 978-1-4391-6799-1
ISBN 978-1-4391-6808-0 (ebook)

For Loretta

We may, indeed, say that the hour of death is uncertain, but when we say this we think of that hour as situated in a vague and remote expanse of time; it does not occur to us that it can have any connection with the day that has already dawned.

—Marcel Proust

Author's Note

I have used as sources for this book the times Della and I spent together, the many letters Della sent to me, and the letters she sent to Judy Ducharme, a woman whom Della considered closer to her than most. Also snapshots and photographs I took, Della took, and Judy took, telephone conversations between Della and myself, conversations with Della's friends, and conversations and events I have taken the liberty of reconstructing, knowing Della as well as I did.

Some names have been changed to protect others' privacy. And no doubt time has eroded my memory for some of the details.

This is the story of Della's life, as close to the truth as I have been able to come, in memory of her. I hope my book will be read as a cautionary tale, an attempt to warn parents and their children of the mistakes my daughter Della and I made. Though I wish it wasn't, this is a true story.

Chuck Barris
October 2008

DELLA

PROLOGUE

My daughter Della was thirty-six years old when she died. Her death certificate said she died from an overdose of drugs and alcohol.

Starting with what Della could remember, like taking her first steps into my arms in a park in Beverly Glen, California, and throughout her short life, Della saw everything as a collection of snapshots. It's weird, but that's how she saw it. After a while, I saw my life the same way.

I took some of those pictures of Della's life. Judy Ducharme, Della's companion since her early childhood, took some too. So did Della. But according to my nonreligious daughter, God was the one who took all the ones we missed, and His photos, according to her, were the best. In her mind, God stood by her side from the day she was born, snapping pictures.

Della described it this way: "He uses His big box camera; a humongous, square black thing. God's camera takes snapshots that don't fall into your hand like Polaroids do. They pop right into your head and stay there forever."

The snapshot of my dead daughter on a couch in her apartment was not a good example of great photography. And wasn't a picture God, or Della, or I took. The snapshot was taken by a police photographer.

If Della were talking about this picture, I imagine she would have said, "I look awful don't I? I know I'm dead, but still . . ."

She does look awful. Her skin is gray. Her body is bone thin. Her eyes have dark circles around them. Her cheeks are sunken. She looks like a Holocaust victim. Her hair had been dyed orange so many times it is beginning to fall out. Imagine, orange hair! Why did she dye her hair orange?

Della would have said, "Because it was my favorite color. Was I weird or was I weird? No, I was stupid. I mean, lying there dead at my age in a frigging police picture says it all, doesn't it?"

Della's three little dogs were probably nearby, sitting around her feet at the far end of the couch. They were alive and well. Just confused and scared to death. The dogs knew Della was dead. Dogs know those things. Della's dogs always slept at her feet when she went to bed at night. If she took a nap on the couch they slept there too.

Tom-the-dog-walker found Della when he came to walk the dogs at eight in the morning. Tom told me no matter how wild Della was the night before, or how often she fell asleep on the couch, she always managed to open one eye in the morning and mumble a greeting to Tom. That morning, she didn't mumble anything. Tom looked at Della closely, shook her shoulders, and when she didn't move, Tom called the police.

In the police picture, the vodka bottle with a small amount of vodka at the bottom is still on the coffee table with all the other detritus. A little cocaine remains in the Ziploc baggie next to the vodka bottle. Della obviously didn't use all the cocaine. Only enough to kill her.

My mother, Della's grandmother, thought Della committed suicide.

"Why would she do that and leave her three dogs behind?" I asked my mother. "Della loved her dogs. I'm sure Della would have thought of her dogs before she did anything like take her life, don't you?"

"No," answered my mother. "Suicidal people don't think about things like who will take care of their dogs when they kill themselves. Suicides don't give a damn about dogs, about themselves, about their parents, about anything. Della was too inconsiderate to think about anything or anyone but herself."

The Los Angeles coroner thought Della ingested too much vodka and cocaine.

I wish the coroner would talk to my mother.

There were two men in Della's life at the time of her death. Tom-the-dog-walker and Strickland-the-dope-peddler. Tom-the-dog-walker was a really nice guy, and a peaceful soul. Strickland-the-dope-peddler was a scumbag and had an aura of violence about him.

Neighbors told the police they could hear Strickland and Della shouting at each other two nights before the dog walker found Della dead. Strickland was a good shouter. He was also good at scoring drugs, but not much good at anything else. I would like to have thought Strickland was guilty of something regarding Della's death, so I could have beaten him within an inch of his life, but I don't think the idiot had anything to do with it, other than contributing drugs, which in itself was major.

After waking up Thursday morning, the day before her death, and seeing what she saw, Della cried out for help. She called Judy Ducharme. Della was sure Judy would come to her apartment and comfort her. Judy was the only "family" Della had in Los Angeles at the time. Judy Ducharme was like a mother to Della. She was someone Della could talk to, and Della needed to talk to someone. Judy would have been able to console her. Judy was good at that.

But Judy was sick and couldn't come.

Della was gone the next morning.

Judy never forgave herself for not coming. It wasn't Judy's fault. She had had the flu and was unable to come. Also, Della's immune system was so weak, Judy would have given Della her flu, and that might have killed Della. I'm sure Della's death, and Judy's inability to get to Della because she was sick when Della needed her, will torment Judy for the rest of her life.

I'm told by friends that Della was very depressed just before she died. Of course she was depressed. She was sick. She was broke. And she was burdened with a low-life lover who provided her with drugs that aided and abetted her depression. Della drank too much vodka, snorted too much cocaine, and died just like the death certificate said she did, from an excessive amount of everything.

I don't think Della wanted to die. I think she made a horrible mistake.

1

Della Charlotte Barris was born at exactly four in the morning, on Christmas Eve 1962.

All the tugboats on the East River blew their foghorns to salute her birth. It was amazing.

I was sitting in the maternity waiting room of New York's Doctors Hospital, waiting for my wife to give birth. My wife's water broke at ten thirty in the evening, the night before Christmas Eve. A taxi driver drove us like a wild man to the hospital. My wife was taken away and I settled in at the maternity waiting room to wait. I was all alone. No other wives were giving birth that Christmas Eve.

The East River was quiet.

At exactly ten after four on Christmas Eve morning, a nurse came into the waiting room. She asked me if I was Mr. Barris. It was a strange question since I was the only man there.

I said I was.

The nurse said, "You are the father of a beautiful baby girl."

"Ten fingers and ten toes?" I asked.

"Ten fingers and ten toes."

"How's my wife?"

"Wonderful."

What a nice word, "wonderful."

I grabbed the nurse and gave her a big hug. I may have even kissed her cheek. And just then, I swear by everything that's holy, all the tugboats on the East River sounded their foghorns. It seemed as though there were a lot of tugboats on the East River that morning. Maybe it was a Christmas Eve tradition for tugs to gather and toot their horns. But at four in the morning? The way I figured it, all those tugs were there to pay tribute to my new daughter. It was really unbelievable. The nurse and I stood staring out the window.

When Della was older, she told me she had heard that story so many times, she was beginning to believe it.

My wife was a very superstitious woman. She didn't want any baby things in the apartment until Della was born. She was worried baby things would jinx her giving birth to a healthy, happy infant. On the second day after Christmas, during one of the busiest shopping days of the year, and in the middle of one of the coldest winters in the history of New York City, I started running all over the place looking for baby things. I had a list that included a bassinet, a crib, diapers, diaper pins, bottles, rubber nipples, baby food, baby formula, and a selection of mobiles, among other things.

No taxis would stop for me standing in the street, holding tons of packages in my arms, a big crib and bassinet leaning against my side. I tried to hide the big items in a Bloomingdale's doorway, then run out and hail a cab. When the cab stopped, I would run back to the doorway, grab the big stuff and the rest of the packages, and run out to the cab. But when I returned to the street, the cab was always gone. I suffered these kinds of trials and tribulations, along with freezing my butt off, until the stores closed.

The second day after Della was born I went to the hospital to visit my wife and new daughter. When I looked through the maternity nursery window, I saw Della in her crib, her little arms pinned to her sides. My daughter was laced up to her neck in a white straitjacket.

The first thing I did was bust into the nursery and check the tiny beaded identification bracelet on Della's wrist to make sure it was my daughter. It was. Then I demanded to see a nurse. The nurse I demanded to see was standing behind me. The nurse placed her hands on my back and pushed me out of the nursery.

In the hall she yelled, "Who do you think you are walking into *my* maternity nursery like that? Do you know the amount of germs and disease you could be carrying? I could have you—"

I yelled back, "Why is my daughter wearing a goddamn straitjacket?"

The nurse yelled, "You just watch your language, sir. Your daughter's wearing the little white coat because she's scratched her cheek with her sharp fingernails. She'll have a scar on her cheek for the rest of her life, and more scars if we—"

"First of all that's *not* a little white coat, it's a straitjacket, and second of all cut her fingernails."

"We cannot cut the baby's fingernails yet. *She's only two days old.*"

"Then I'm taking my daughter home."

"Oh no you're not," said the nurse.

"Oh yes I am."

And that's exactly what I did. I went down to my wife's room, told her to get out of bed and pack her things, she and the baby were going home.

My wife said, "What?"

I went back to the nursery, walked in, and bundled Della up. The two of us went to collect my wife and another blanket for Della. Then the three of us walked out of the hospital's main entrance and hailed a cab. We took the taxi to our apartment on East Fifty-fifth Street.

It was minus two degrees outside that morning.

There's a framed photograph of Della taken in January or February 1962, when she was a couple of weeks old, a month at most, that used to hang on my bedroom wall. In the picture, Della is lying on top of a diaper on my lap. My legs were stretched out in front of me, crossed at the ankles. It was early on a cold winter morning. I was giving Della her five a.m. feeding. I always took the five a.m. feeding, so my wife could sleep through the night. Della's mother was responsible for the rest of the feedings except for ten o'clock at night. I took that one too so my wife could go to bed. She was usually exhausted by ten o'clock. Babies were on a tight feeding schedule in those days.

I can still remember the horrendous alarm clock on my bedside table. It had a grotesque ring. That ring felt as though it were going off *inside* my ear. I dreaded that alarm. It rang at the ungodly hour of 4:45 a.m. I would wake a half hour before it went off and wait in terror for it to clang. It was catastrophic for me to get out of that warm, snuggly bed during those freezing New York winter mornings. At least I thought so while I was getting out of bed.

When the alarm went off, I would stall and stall, telling myself that I was sure kids in India and China weren't all fed at five a.m. Think of the thousands of Chinese and Indian kids who must have missed their five a.m. feedings and survived. But I wasn't 100 percent sure they survived, so I got out of bed, pulled a sweatshirt over my pajamas, put a woolen robe over that, and staggered to the kitchen. There I would turn the fire on under a pot of water and wait for the water to boil. I would take a bottle of Della's formula from the fridge and stand it up in the pot of boiling water so that the bottle's rubber nipple wouldn't get wet. I'd wait two or three minutes, shake some of the milk on my wrist, palm up, to see if the formula was okay to drink. Then I'd go back to our bedroom, pull the soundly sleeping Della from her crib, wrap all her covers and blankets around her, and take her and the bottle to the living room, saying things like, "I don't like this any more than you do, Della honey."

In the living room, I'd sit down in my favorite armchair, a big, soft old green thing, hold Della in the crook of my arm, and feed her the bottle of formula. Della's big blue eyes would lock on to mine and never look away. Never. It was the most incredible phenomenon. Once I got past the alarm clock, I remember those early-morning feedings as being some of the sweetest moments of my life.

When my daughter finished her bottle, I would turn her on her stomach, place her on my legs on a spare diaper in case she spit some up, which was usually the case, and pat her back until she burped. Eventually when she did, I'd say, "That's a good girl," as if she were a little dog who was paper trained, and wipe her mouth with the diaper. Then I'd sit with her for another half hour or so, patting and stroking her warm little back under her nightshirt and blankets.

The photograph is in an ornate antique frame that used to hang in my bedroom. Della had probably just burped. She looks relieved. In the picture her head is as bald as a billiard ball, her lips are concave like a toothless old man's, and her eyes are wide as saucers. There is some drool coming out of the right corner of her mouth. Her wee chin is resting on my leg, and her cheeks are puffed out to the sides like a chipmunk's filled with nuts.

When I looked at it, I would remember Della lying on my knee with that sweet face of hers and wonder where it all went wrong. I'd start asking myself dozens of questions that troubled me, questions like, Did it start to go wrong when Della's mother and I were divorced? Or when Della and her mother left for Switzerland and her mother enrolled Della in the *école*? Or when I was awarded custody of Della? Or when I sent Della to Beverly Hills High School? Or was it when Della was sixteen and I gave her plenty of money, then threw her out of the house and told her not to come back until she was drug free? It could be all of the above, or none of the above.

After a while I grew very tired of asking myself those questions and took the picture down from the wall.

There's a snapshot I took the time I taught Della how to walk. I guess it was late 1963 or early 1964 when Della was a year old, maybe older. I can't remember her exact age but I can remember that day as if it happened an hour ago.

I had just transferred from New York to Los Angeles with a new job and a long title: Director of Daytime Television, West Coast Division, American Broadcasting Company. The three of us were living in an apartment building on the Sunset Strip in Hollywood. The apartment building was loaded with hookers. Nice girls, but hookers. I was a tad concerned but Della loved them and they loved Della. The hookers would lovingly pinch her, and hug her, and "kitchey-coo" her constantly with their fingers under her chin.

One beautiful Saturday morning I took Della to Beverly Glen Park. Every warm and sunny Saturday and Sunday morning the locals would stream into the park and immediately grab hunks of lawn to call their own. It was a big park with lots of people who couldn't or wouldn't go to the beach. Fortunately there was plenty of room.

Everyone brought beach towels, folding chairs, or small back rests. Everyone lathered themselves from head to toe with various suntan lotions. Some held reflectors under their chins. Everybody faced the sun as though the sun were Mecca. There were lots of little babies, kids, and dogs. Everyone looked average. Just working people. Same as me.

I remember taking the picture of the two of us in the park. I set the camera on self-timer, placed it on an empty bench, and walked a few feet away. I held Della in the crook of my right arm and gripped a carryall in my left hand. While we waited for the camera to snap, I told Della to say "cheese." I remember Della looking at me with a very annoyed expression on her face.

My daughter was wearing a pair of thin fire-engine-red Dr.

Denton jammies. The jammies went from her neck all the way
down to the ends of her toes. The rear end of her jammies was
packed with diapers. I dressed her. In the picture Della looks
embarrassed. She thinks she's the laughingstock of the park.

I carried Della to a place on the grass where we had some
room and placed her on her wobbly legs. I ran a few feet away,
got down on my knees, stretched out my arms, grinned from
ear to ear like an idiot, and motioned for Della to come to me.
Della started out, took a step or two, then suddenly sat down on
her well-padded bum. I ran back to her as quickly as I could, all
hyperactive and extra jolly, and said, "That's okay, Della, that's
okay. You did great. Just great. Don't worry about a thing.
We'll try again, okay?"

Della didn't know what the hell I was talking about.

I lifted her up, held her close to my chest, patted her back
a couple of times, whispered some mumbo jumbo in her ear,
stood her on her feet again, and took off.

I ran back to where I'd come from, got down on my knees,
held out my arms, grinned like an idiot again, and encouraged
Della to come to me. Della grinned back. She grinned a lot
lately. Della had two teeth on her bottom gum, which she loved
to flaunt.

Della started walking toward me, her hands straight out in
front of her, fingers splayed. She staggered along like a blind-
folded drunk playing pin the tail on the donkey. She was laughing so hard her face was red as a beet. I had no idea why she was
laughing.

Della took one tentative step, then another, and then she went
plop on her bum again. Every time Della went plop, I would race
over to her, say something stupid that I was glad she didn't un-

derstand, stand her back up on her fat, wobbly legs, run quickly back to where I'd come from, get down on my knees again, stick out my arms again, grin, and ask her to come to me one more time. Della appeared confused at my gibberish, started out, fell down, and laughed her ass off.

That's how we spent the morning. Della taking a few steps, falling down, and laughing her ass off. Me running to her, standing her up, running a short distance away, grinning my cretin grin, then watching her fall down.

After what seemed like a zillion failures, Della took two large steps, then three, then four, staggered a little bit, then five, then six, almost fell but didn't . . . then seven . . . eight . . . ten steps and she was in my arms. She had just walked. My God, she walked. It was one of the happiest moments in my life. I was ecstatic. I picked Della up and whirled her around and around in a circle. Her little legs were sticking straight out behind her.

"Della," I said, "you walked. You took your very first steps. And you did it with me! You did it with me! Always remember, honey, just like now, I'll always be there to catch you when you fall."

As it turned out I wasn't.

We moved from our apartment on the Sunset Strip to a house in Encino, in the San Fernando Valley. There's a snapshot of Della and me standing by the swimming pool of our new house. It was the first house I ever owned, *and* it had a swimming pool. It was a small one but it was a swimming pool just the same.

Because of my wife's strange desire to entertain our neighbors every weekend, I would spend hours at the hardware store on Saturday afternoons, examining nails and power saws and screwdrivers and wrenches as if those things never existed before. Most Saturdays I would take Della with me to the hardware store. We would return carrying bags filled with all sorts of new tools, nails, and screws. I would place the brand-new tools beside the old (new) tools on shelves I found on one of the garage walls. Then I'd place the nails and screws in plastic boxes, label the boxes, and line them up in neat rows on those shelves. It was a whole new way of life for me.

I soon had a routine. Every Sunday I mowed the small lawn in front of our house. When I mowed the lawn I used a new power mower I'd bought at the hardware store. I'd never mowed a lawn before in my life because I grew up in center-city Philadelphia. I swore to my wife I loved mowing our front lawn. She didn't believe me. She told me I was going to blow a gasket someday soon.

"It won't last long," my wife told Della. "One day he'll explode."

I think Della and her mother were hoping I would explode soon. I was becoming a raging bore playing Lord of the Manor.

Our house had practically no backyard. That's mainly why the pool was so small. If you stood on the sidewalk and faced the front door, our pool was on the right side of the house toward the rear. It was an egg-shaped pool, five feet deep at the deep end. The pool was surrounded by a square of cement. Bordering the cement was a waist-high chain-link fence with a latched gate that only a mechanical engineer could open. Inside the fence were a multitude of wooden lounge chairs, with wooden footrests that hooked on to the chairs and thick pads that ran the length of the chair and footrest. The chairs surrounded the pool. I told Della's mother we had too many lounge chairs for such a tiny pool. "Our pool looks like the deck of a cruise ship."

My wife didn't hear a word I said.

While I played weekend handyman and gardener, my wife enjoyed being the Hostess with the Mostess. She would entertain everyone on the block who didn't have pools, including the obnoxious Lipshitz family, our repulsive neighbors, who *did* have a pool. They just didn't want to mess it up. The Lipshitz family were at our pool every weekend. To me, the most loathsome sight of all was the Lipshitz daughters. Two teenage girls who sat on lounge chairs all day long, on either side of their portable radio, and listened to blaring rock music. The most amazing thing of all was that nobody, not my wife, not even me, ever told the pimply-faced Lipshitz sisters to turn their damn radio down or leave the radio home when they came to our pool. Being neighborly was new to us. So my wife and I just suffered.

One family had a fox terrier they actually called Bowser. They brought Bowser along every time they came to our pool. Bowser never stopped barking. Another couple, the Donnleys, had a newborn baby girl named Hester. (I didn't think any girl had been named Hester since Hester Prynne in *The Scarlet Letter*.) Baby Hester howled when she was awake. If she wasn't howling she was pooping. Mr. and Mrs. Donnley were forever cleaning up baby Hester's horrendous-looking poops at poolside. This is why I would spend hours at the hardware store every Saturday and mowed my microscopic lawn as long as I could on Sunday afternoon in the scorching sun. Anything was better than cooling off in my pool with our revolting neighbors.

All through the weekends my wife would bring out piles of hot towels fresh from the dryer for our nauseating guests. My wife worked like a dog producing the hot towels all afternoon. I constantly asked her why she felt it necessary to keep the neighborhood in hot towels. Particularly when her beloved neighbors were taking advantage of her.

"How? How are they taking advantage of me?"

"I saw Mrs. Donnley use one of your fresh towels to wipe baby Hester's behind. It was an extremely disgusting sight."

My wife immediately cut down on her hot towel production.

When Della was two years old she was as cute as a bug's ear. She had little bow lips, a longish nose that came from thousands of years of Jewish breeding. (I happened to adore her nose.) She had big blue eyes, a potbelly, and very fat legs with deep creases around them. She had white blond hair, so blond her eyebrows disappeared. In the picture by the pool my wife took, Della's wearing only the blue bottoms of her bikini bathing suit. I'm bending over her so I could have my arm around her little shoulders and be in the picture. I'm in my early thirties.

One Sunday I was mowing the front lawn. The usual mob of neighbors was at our pool. Because of where the house was situated, the pool crowd was unable to see our front lawn.

Suddenly my wife sat bolt upright in her lounge chair and said, "He's not mowing the lawn."

She was right. The sound of the lawn mower going back and forth had stopped. The mowing sound might have stopped hours ago, but because of the Lipshitz sisters' blaring radio, none of the guests around the pool could hear much of anything. But my wife could. Seconds after she realized there wasn't any mowing, she picked Della up and ran to the front of our house. The lawn mower was there, but I wasn't. Nor was my car.

"I told you he'd snap someday," Della's mother said to her. According to Della, her mother was extraordinarily calm about everything.

I never returned to that house in Encino. I went to Hollywood and rented a furnished apartment in the same apartment building on the Sunset Strip we had lived in when we first came to California, the one with all the hookers who loved Della. I phoned my wife and told her where to come. At least an apartment house full of hookers was better than living next door to the Lipshitz family.

Della's mother made all the arrangements for the sale of the Encino house. She supervised the packing and moving of our furniture into storage. I don't remember my wife saying a word about the crazy stunt I pulled, pro or con, nor did she ever ask me to explain why I did what I did. I guess it was Bowser's barking, Hester Donnley's yellow poops, and the Lipshitz sisters' blaring radio that tossed me over the edge and made me flee the burbs.

Della had another favorite snapshot. In it she is standing in front of her Montessori school with three of her best friends. They have their arms around one another's shoulders, but you can't see that in the photograph. You can only see their four faces. Heads touching heads. I took the picture on their first day of school. They were all six years old. They all knew one another before they came to the Montessori school in Hollywood. The school building is behind them, but you can't see it.

The four kids celebrated Christmas at one another's houses and had Easter egg hunts together on their lawns. During Halloween they went door to door yelling, "Trick or treat, smell my feet, give us something good to eat." When it was Toby's birthday, the three girls would sing to him: "Happy birthday to you. You live in a zoo. You look like a monkey, and smell like one too." Then the girls would giggle like crazy.

One of the girls was Turkish. Her name was Medva. The other girl was black. Her name was Bonnie. The third best friend of Della's, Toby, was Mexican. Toby had a great head of jet black hair and was cute as hell. Della had a crush on him before she knew what crushes were. I've forgotten all their last names. All I remember is that the four of them stuck together and always seemed to be having fun.

It was 1968. Della was five years old. There was a war going on in some place called Vietnam. It seemed that most of the kids in Della's school were against the war. That's because most of their parents were hippies and were always yelling, "Make love, not war."

My wife was a hippie. At least she was in the sixties. She wore long dresses and laced-up boots and lots of peace signs on braided leather thongs around her neck. (At times I even wore a Nehru jacket.) My wife was definitely against the war. So was I. And so, it seemed, were all of our friends, at least those who sent their kids to the Montessori school.

I eventually made a huge poster using that picture of Della and her three friends on their first day of school. The poster was as big as a large American flag with red and white stripes where the stripes belonged. In the square where the stars were supposed to be, I used the picture of the four kids' heads. If you're looking at the poster straight on, the Mexican boy, Toby, was on the left. Then came my little blond-headed daughter, then Medva's soft tan Turkish face, and next to her black Bonnie. All four were laughing, probably at something one of them had just said.

The poster hit a patriotic nerve. It had nowhere near the impact of the Marines raising the flag on Iwo Jima, but it was a big winner nonetheless. The poster started showing up all over the place. It was copied and recopied. They said there was something like a million of these flag posters all over the world. It was even a huge seller at Woodstock in 1969, a year later.

Shortly after I launched the poster, my wife and I decided to end our marriage. We had been arguing a lot. No, more than a lot. All the time. Fuzzy arguments that circled around the same accusations. We hurled identical sentences at each other endlessly, for over a year.

"You've been seeing someone else."

"No, *you've* been seeing someone else."

"Everything's an argument with you."

"Everything's an argument with *you.*"

"You're driving me crazy."

"No, *you're* driving *me* crazy."

Back and forth like a broken record. It must have been sickening to listen to, and the only one listening to our arguments was Della. All our battles started the same way, a seemingly minor misunderstanding, and ended up the same way, with one of us storming out of the house furious and driving off in his or her automobile. I know Della couldn't stand watching or listening to us argue. Della would run to her room, get in her closet, and close the door. After about a year of constant combat we agreed to part for good and always.

A few years earlier, I had left the American Broadcasting Company and started a little production company of my own, and it was doing very well. I had created two new game shows that seemed to be hits: *The Dating Game* and *The Newlywed Game*. Della's mother came from a fairly wealthy family, so money wasn't an issue for either one of us. What was an issue was the gentle fabric of our family, which was about to be torn to shreds. When my wife and I divorced, I believe we destroyed a big part of something hugely important to our daughter.

It was a bright and sunny afternoon in the summer, about fourish I think, when I moved out of our home. I spent the entire day piling my possessions into my secondhand car, a white Buick Skylark convertible with black leather interior and a black roof. The roof was down that afternoon so I could fit all of my personal possessions inside. It was a time when I could get everything I owned into a small convertible automobile.

On the morning I moved out of the house, Della woke up sick to her stomach. She started throwing up when I began putting my belongings into the automobile. On more than one occasion I heard Della vomiting in the downstairs bathroom. I felt horrible but did nothing about it. I had made the decision to leave, and on that pretty morning I was going to leave.

Della tried to stop me. It seemed as if it was a matter of life or death for her. Maybe it was. She grabbed me around my waist and screamed, "Don't leave, Daddy! Please don't leave!"

My wife looked at me, blew smoke out of her lungs, and said,

"You're breaking your daughter's heart and tearing this household apart, you know that, don't you?"

I thought that was a stupid thing to say. I would have thought Della's mother would be calming Della, telling her something like, "This entire divorce thing is between your father and me. It has nothing to do with you, Della. Your father and I love you more than anything in the world, and your daddy is going to be seeing you just like before. Don't think you're to blame for any of this." Or something like that, instead of standing in a corner with her arms crossed, smoking a cigarette and saying, "You're breaking your daughter's heart." My soon-to-be ex-wife was making the nightmare worse. Much worse.

"You don't love us anymore, do you, Daddy?"

"Of course I do. I will always love you, Della. Always."

Della's arms had slipped down my legs to my shins. I tried to pry her arms away from my legs without hurting her but couldn't. I said, "Come on, Della, cut it out. Stop crying and let me go. Cut it out, Della."

I continued walking to the door, dragging Della along the floor behind me. It was an awful scene and a terrible moment in my life, one I try constantly to forget. Slowly Della's arms slid down my shins so that she ended up holding the bottom of one foot. I tried to jerk my foot out of her hands. When I did the heel of my shoe hit her jaw. Della howled. The afternoon was becoming a nightmare. I knelt down and took Della in my arms and said, "I'm sorry, honey. I'm so sorry."

When Della stopped crying I stood up and started for the door again.

Della screamed, "Daddy, please don't leave. Please don't go."

I ignored her and walked to the front door. I remember

Della's mother leaning against a wall on the other side of the room. She stood with her arms still crossed over her chest, the same cigarette still between her lips, one eye closed by the smoke, a furious expression still on her face. I also remember Della's sobbing, "Daddy, Daddy," on the floor. It was a scene I don't think I'll ever forget my entire life. It's one of God's photographs. Perhaps his cruelest.

2

It's 1970. Richard Milhous Nixon had been president for a year.

It was Della's mother's idea. She began thinking about pulling Della out of school so the two of them could move to Europe. Politically it was a bad year for Della's mother and her friends. The Vietnam War, Nixon. Things weren't right in America. So when Della's mother announced she was moving to Switzerland, her hippie buddies said, "Wow" and "No kidding" when she talked about becoming an expatriate. Della's mother loved her new celebrity status. She basked in it for five minutes or so. The woman had the bizarre notion that moving to Europe was daring, doing the thing her friends wanted to do but either couldn't afford to or didn't have the nerve to do. My ex-wife thought she was showing everyone she had the courage of her convictions. She was convinced everybody would think of her as a gutsy woman who was putting her money where her mouth was. In all honesty, I don't think any of her friends gave a hoot about her guts or where she put her money.

Della told me when her mother wasn't taking care of her, she was spending all her time at home entertaining her hippie friends and smoking a lot of grass. Della said all her mother's crowd ever talked about was how awful Nixon was. I sometimes wondered if Della was telling me what she thought I wanted to hear. I also wondered if she was doing the same with her mother.

Della said, "Every time I ask Mom why we're leaving America, she says, 'Nixon.'"

I don't think my ex-wife was moving to Switzerland because of Nixon or any other political ideas. She wasn't a political radical. I think the *real* reason my ex-wife and Della were leaving the country was because Della's mother was upset about our divorce. She was embarrassed to be dating again at that time in her life. She was upset because now she couldn't leave for work anymore with me in the morning and program the music for my game shows. Now she would have to stay home all day and take care of our daughter. She would have to stay home with her daughter in Geneva too, but at least she wouldn't feel the pressure to date. She would have to do something drastic like moving away or her new life would drive her batty. I think that's why she decided to make Della and herself expats.

I wondered if Della's mother thought out the consequences of taking Della to Europe, of pulling her out of the school she loved, taking her away from her best friends, her cozy home, and comfy bed. No matter how hard I pleaded, she wouldn't listen to me. Or Della. Eventually she forbade both of us from talking

about the two of them staying in America. Della's mother made
that very clear. She told me I was interfering with her life. And
then I thought, The two of them will be less of a problem to me
in Europe than in America. So I stopped fighting it.

I think Della's mother boasted so much about leaving the
United States that she eventually *had* to go. In the middle of
Nixon's third year the two left for Switzerland. The funny thing
is, if Della's mother had waited a little longer, President Nixon,
the object of her supposed dissatisfaction, would have been
gone.

My ex-wife rented a chalet. It seemed that all the chalets in
Switzerland had names. Theirs was called the Villa Clairvue.
Their address was Route de Founex, 1296 Coppet (VD), Switzerland. Coppet was a section of Geneva. The chalet she rented
was at the top of a steep, muddy, unpaved street. It was muddy
and unpaved because a lot of construction was going on. Apartment houses were going up, along with an addition to a United
Nations building. The building was just down the street from
their chalet. Della's mother wrote home and told all her friends
about the UN building. Della thought the UN building was a
big so-what. Her mother's friends probably did too.

Della telephoned me and said, "The weather here in Switzerland's awful. It's nothing like California. It's always raining and it's always cold. You have to wear tons of sweaters and
jackets just to stay warm and dry. And it's always dark in the
chalet, mainly because the place is filled with weird lamps that
have the dimmest twenty-five-watt bulbs ever made. And ugly
long cords coming from the lamps' tops, not their bottoms. And
another thing. The apartment's furnished with the most uncomfortable stick furniture ever made. And there's really strange art

on the walls. The bathroom's nothing like the one we had in Hollywood. For one thing it has a big useless old bidet. Big deal. I use the bidet to clean the mud off my boots."

I said, "I don't think you should do that."

"Yeah, well . . . anyway, the shower has a long metal cord that looks like a gas pump with a nozzle attached to one end. You hold the nozzle in your hand and spray yourself. You fix the temperature of the water with one knob. It took me a week and a half to get the water temperature right. And then if Mom flushes her toilet while I'm in the shower, I'm either burned alive or I freeze to death. The big attraction about the chalet, according to the real estate agent, is that Mom and I can see the snow-covered crown of Mont Blanc from our living room window. Big deal. As far as I'm concerned, you see the top of one snow-covered mountain, you've seen 'em all. But Mom is impressed."

"What do you do for breakfast? They don't have any coffee shops like Duke's, do they?"

"Every morning we walk to the InterContinental Hotel for breakfast. We go to the InterContinental because they speak English there. Mom likes to understand what the waiters are saying. She also loves to smoke in the dining room. Everybody smokes everywhere in Europe. It's so smoky in the dining room of the InterContinental Hotel, it's like walking into a billiard parlor."

"When have you ever walked into a billiard parlor?"

"Anyway, Mom loves it. She also loves the feeling of being an expat. She likes reading her *Herald Tribune* and drinking the awful-tasting mud Europeans call coffee. As for me, I miss the good old US of A. And I miss you. You're my favorite person in the whole world. Judy's next. Mom's third."

In 1972, shortly after they began living in Switzerland, Della was enrolled in a private boarding school in Vevey, near the small town of Versoix. Versoix is above Lake Geneva, up in the hills, and supposedly dates back to Roman times. It looks it. Della telephoned me to say, "The first time I saw my new school was on a cold, gray, rainy day. I remembered being bummed when I saw it. My new school looked nothing like my old Montessori school back home. The miserable weather, the old buildings all made me depressed. I missed my best friends Medva, Bonnie, and Toby something awful. One of God's snapshots I'll never forget is the one He took of me looking out of my mom's automobile window the day I first saw that awful school. The only time I felt worse was the day you left home."

"It can't be *that* bad, Della."

"It is," she said. "Vevey is supposed to be cute and quaint. I think it's more like dilapidated and rickety. There isn't anything about the town I like, not even its world-famous Musée Suisse de l'Appareil Photographique, which, according to one of my teachers, is the only museum of its kind in Switzerland. As far as I'm concerned it's just another dumb old photography place. The *musée* has a lot of ancient photographs of dead people and old masters in it. 'Dead' and 'old,' two words that sum up Europe to me."

"Look at the good side, Della. Europe is full of culture."

"Culture smulture, Daddy. Europe is old and grungy. Mainly old. Take the village of Vevey. It's old, old, old, and *that's* supposed to be charming? I don't think it's charming at all. I think it's grungy."

"Is there anything *not* grungy about the town? Isn't there *anything* nice?"

"Not really. Well, Vevey is at the foot of Mont Pèlerin, Daddy. Mont Pèlerin is a small mountain with some snow at the top. That's kind of nice. But in all honesty, the mountain's nothing to write home about. But it *does* become half decent when you're skiing down it. I gotta tell you, Daddy, everything in Switzerland, like I said, is so old, it's pathetic. And of all the miserable sights in Versoix, the worst is our school. The place reminds me of a penitentiary. Breakfast is served at seven a.m. sharp, lunch at precisely twelve sharp, dinner at six sharp. You know how punctual the stupid Swiss are, with their clocks and everything. Sharp means sharp. We have classes from eight in the morning until four in the afternoon with an hour off for lunch. Chapel on Sunday is mandatory. Our penitentiary is supposed to be nondenominational, but in truth the service on Sunday is very Catholic. Switzerland is predominantly a Catholic country, and the family who donated the school to the town were heavy into Catholicism. Which I don't mind. Oddly enough I love all that Catholic bugaboo."

"That's strange," I said.

"It's true, Daddy, I do. Anyway the students here at the penitentiary are mostly the spoiled kids of rich, bored parents. The mothers and fathers never have time for the kids they leave here, or they couldn't control them and gave up. When you come to visit me you'll see exactly what I mean. Most of the students here at the penitentiary were placed here so their parents could travel and play around as if they didn't have any kids at all."

On one of Della's vacations she told me about skiing at her school.

"The most important extracurricular activity at the penitentiary is skiing."

"Must you call your school a penitentiary?"

"Well, it is. Anyway, the school really loves their skiers. I hate skiing, even though I'm pretty good at it. What I despise most of all is putting on all my ski clothes. I mean, just getting my ski boots laced up is a big deal. Then climbing onto the damn windy lift, riding up to the top of the freezing mountain, and then having to pee. Which happens all the time as soon as you get to the top. You know what I do? I just pee in my pants. We all do. All the girls. It's hard winning medals skiing in clothes soaked with freezing pee, Daddy, but I did. I ended up really liking to ski. You feel so free when you ski. At least I do. I love when skiing gets scary. I'm kind of a daredevil on skis. I'm fearless. I can't go fast enough. I mean, so what if I break a leg? I just wouldn't have to go to school, would I. And all the girls would talk about me, wouldn't they? Anyway, I ended up winning three medals during our last intraschool competition. All of them as a downhill racer. I'm the fastest skier at the stupid *école*. I just don't care about anything when I'm up on skis, Daddy."

Della was ten years old when she won those medals.

There's a snapshot of Della lying in a hospital bed. She asked a nurse to take the photograph. Della's dressed in a hospital gown, her eyes are closed, and her tongue is hanging out of the side of her mouth. She's trying not to smile. Della's sense of humor. I must say, she looks cute as a button.

You can't see what a miserable day it is but Della said it had been raining for weeks.

Six months after she arrived at her new school, Della be-

came sick. When she turned yellow the school authorities sent
her to a hospital in Geneva. I don't remember which hospital
it was, just that it was a Catholic hospital. The nurses all wore
gray uniforms, gray caps, and white capes over their shoulders
and down their backs. According to Della, all the nurses had
extremely large silver or gold crosses around their necks, and
they were all nuns. Della was in a semiprivate room. There
was an old man in the bed next to her. You can't see him in
the photo; he's too far to the left. Della called him Old Man
Mose.

A nurse told Della, "The dear man will be going to his eter-
nal rest shortly."

Occasionally Della would see Old Man Mose when the
nurses and doctors had to do something to him and they forgot to pull the curtain closed. The old man's face was already
skull-like, his cheeks sunken, nose thin and beaky, his white
hair wispy. Della said Old Man Mose's hair looked like loose
bird feathers.

His fragile, bony hands were always outside the covers. That's
where the nurses put them and that's where they stayed. Della
said it looked as though you could snap off Old Man Mose's
fingers as easily as breaking a pretzel stick. She said Old Man
Mose *never* moved. There were huge needles sticking into both
of Old Man Mose's hands, kept there with white adhesive tape.
The needles were attached to long clear plastic tubes running up
to bags of different liquids. The bags hung from chrome stands
on wheels. The old geezer was wearing the same gown Della
was wearing. It was green and white checked. You tied it at the
neck and waist.

One morning Della telephoned to tell me she watched a

priest enter the closed curtains next to the old man's bed during the night. The next morning when she woke up, Old Man Mose was gone. The curtain was pulled open. The bed was flat as a board with fresh white sheets on it. A green hospital blanket was folded in a small square at the foot of the bed. The nurses told Della the old man had died during the night. They had taken Old Man Mose away while Della was sleeping.

Della said she told a nurse, "Nobody ever came to visit Old Man Mose while he was in the hospital, at least not while I was here. Nobody sent him a get-well card, or flowers, or candy. Nobody sent me anything either. And now Old Man Mose is gone. I hope to Jesus I don't die that way, all alone."

Unfortunately she would.

Della told me after Old Man Mose died, she had this conversation with one of the nurses:

"Della, stop taking the Lord's name in vain. You repeatedly take the Lord's name in vain."

"Okay. But goddamn it, will anybody remember Old Man Mose a week from now? Will you nurses who cared for him remember him? Will anybody remember me?"

"The Lord will," said the nurse.

"What will happen if I die? Will the priest come in to see me and recite some mumbo jumbo?"

"The priest doesn't recite mumbo jumbo," said the nurse. "He gives the person their last rites."

"Will the priest give me my last rites?"

"Certainly, dear."

"But I'm not Catholic. I'm Jewish."

"Then Father Murphy won't give you anything," said the nurse.

Della woke one morning to waves of rain beating against her hospital room window. Even though it was morning, it was so dark and gray outside Della had to turn on the lamp on the table by her bed. The lamp had a twenty-five-watt bulb in it that made her room more depressing than it already was.

"Why," she asked the nurse, "do all the damn lamps in Europe have twenty-five-watt bulbs in them? At night this hospital room is the gloomiest place imaginable."

"Do you believe in God, child?" asked the nurse.

"Not really."

"Well," said the nurse, "start believing in Jesus Christ our Savior and your room will light up. Mark my words."

Della told me, "Was that an answer or was that an answer?"

Della wrote she felt sick to her stomach constantly. All she wanted to do was either throw up or sleep. It was her third day in the hospital. There was a sign on her door that said QUARANTINE. Nobody replaced Old Man Mose in the other bed. Her breakfast tray arrived with the usual garbage: a cup of awful-tasting tea, a cold soft-boiled egg, and a piece of burnt, rock-hard toast.

Della said to the nurse, "If I start believing in God will my breakfasts get better?"

"Mind your mouth," answered the nurse.

Della told me at the start of the fourth day in the hospital, she began to feel very sorry for herself, and afraid. She said she felt extra miserable being sick in a foreign city, and alone. And Della was alone. Her mother was in Greece or somewhere, Judy Ducharme was unavailable, and I was working in Los Angeles. The morning of the fourth day in the hospital was an all-time low for Della's spirits.

She told me she would put herself to sleep at night dreaming she lived in a big house with extra-loving and sensationally good-looking parents. They weren't her mother or me. They were make-believe parents. How sad is that?

She also had five make-believe handsome brothers and five make-believe really pretty sisters. All of her brothers and sisters were the most popular kids in Della's make-believe high school. Della was very popular too. The make-believe high school was somewhere in the United States, someplace where it was sunny all the time (probably California). Della's brothers were star athletes and some of her sisters were cheerleaders. Della was the baby of the family. Her sisters and brothers ranged in age from thirteen to eighteen. (There may have been some age duplication in there somewhere.) Della's brothers and sisters all went to the same junior and senior high school, which was all one school but spread over a beautiful campus. Della was in the junior high part of the school. Medva, Bonnie, and Toby were in her class.

All of Della's friends envied Della's family.

Della's brothers and sisters doted on Della. So did her dream parents. Occasionally Della would get into trouble. Nothing terribly bad; no drugs, or cigarettes, or alcohol, or skipping classes, nothing like that. Just normal mischief. Della was a mischievous little girl. Most of the time when Della's dream parents were chastising her, she could hear her dream brothers and sisters chuckling lovingly in the background. Della told me about her dream family months after she got out of the hospital. Even about her dream parents. She said she loved the dream so much, she couldn't wait to go to sleep at night.

And then one morning I walked into Della's hospital room.

Della was so happy to see me, she started sobbing. When she did, I got this terrible pang in my chest, or heart, or stomach; somewhere on my person. An awful sickness spread over me. I was suddenly sick about Della's life. It was so sad how alone she was, and how frightened and pitiful. My leaving home and our divorce had caused Della such terrible pain. The move to Switzerland. Her new school. Had it caused us, her mother and me, as much pain? Not even close.

"Daddy. I'm so glad you came," Della said through her tears.

"Hi, sweetie. I'd give you a big hug but I don't want to catch what you have."

"What *do* I have?"

"Hepatitis."

"Is that bad?"

"Not the kind you have. You'll be fine in a couple of weeks."

"When will I be able to go back to school?"

"I'm not sure."

"How do you catch hepa . . . hepa . . ."

"Probably from something you ate."

"I'm so happy to see you, Daddy." She began crying again.

"Now stop that crying."

"Okay," Della said. "It's just . . . okay . . . I'll stop crying."

I took off my raincoat and rain hat, shook them out, and hung them up on a coat hook.

We talked for hours and hours. I left the hospital to get some dinner. I told Della I'd return that evening. I went back to a hotel near the hospital whose name I forget. The restaurant and bar were on the top floor of the hotel with a panoramic view of Geneva. I drank a couple of scotch and sodas. And then a couple more.

The next morning a nurse handed Della a note. It was from me. The note said I had urgent business to attend to, that I loved Della more than anything in the whole world, and that I'd see her real soon.

I wouldn't see Della for six months.

3

During a school holiday, Della and I spent time together in Lausanne, Switzerland. When she started at the *école,* the students were all girls. The word was, boys were coming to the *école.* Until then, the girls dated boys from the town, whom they called "locals."

Della told me, "The grades at the *école* went from first to twelfth. You didn't room by grades. You roomed with whomever you wanted to room with. If you couldn't think of someone, or didn't know anybody, you were assigned a roommate. I was put in a room with another American girl four years older than me."

Della showed me a snapshot of her and her roommate. The two girls were standing together in front of the mansion that was their dormitory. The roommate had her arm around Della's shoulders. Her roommate was tall and gangly looking. She was on crutches. She had one leg in a cast. The roommate came from

Vermont. She and Della were two of the dozen or so Americans at the school.

When this picture was taken, Della's roommate was five feet ten inches tall, and growing. She had a pretty face, big brown eyes, and a button nose. She towered over everyone in the school. Later, when boys entered the *école*, Della's roommate was bigger than all of them. I think Della's roommate would have been really popular if she hadn't been so tall. Her height caused her all sorts of problems, most of them psychological. None of the new boys wanted to go out with an Amazon. They all ignored Della's roommate.

Della called her roommate the Vermontster behind her back. (I never did find out the roommate's real name.) Della told me the Vermontster had some very strange habits. She said "golly" and "I mean" a lot and was constantly repeating sentences she had already said. She also held her head tilted to the side like a sparrow.

Della's roommate had broken her ankle skiing. Della said that's why she was on crutches. The crutches didn't fit her; they were too small, but they were the only ones the infirmary had left. There must have been a lot of skiing accidents that week. Della was convinced her roommate liked being on small crutches. They made her stand bent over, which made the Vermontster smaller. The Vermontster was on crutches until the day she left school. When she graduated, word got around that her parents had her committed to a drug rehabilitation hospital.

"We're all a bunch of square pegs trying to get into round holes" was something Della said about her classmates. I never forgot it.

The Vermontster and Della shared a large room with a beamed ceiling and a bay window. They each had a bed, a bureau, a desk, a desk lamp, and a closet. The bathroom was down the hall. Della told me she and the Vermontster had this conversation:

"Golly, Della," said the Vermontster, "so how come you ended up here? How come you ended up here, huh? I mean, why did your parents pick *this* dump? Didn't they know about its reputation? Didn't your parents check out the school's reputation?"

"My mother and father got a divorce," Della said. "My mother kept me and we moved from Los Angeles to Geneva. I have no idea why my mother picked this dump."

"Why?"

"Why what? Why did we move? My mother didn't like President Nixon."

"No. Why did your parents get divorced? What made them get divorced?"

"I guess they stopped liking each other," Della said. "Why do people usually get divorced?"

Della told me her roommate's parents were divorced. Divorce was a subject that seemed to fascinate most of the kids at Della's school.

"Did you live close to Hollywood?" asked the Vermontster, her head tilted to the side. "I mean, I read everything I can about Hollywood. How close did you live to Hollywood?"

"We lived *in* Hollywood," Della said.

"Gol-lee! *In* Hollywood? In *Hollywood*! Jesus, why would anyone want to leave there? I mean, why would anyone move from Hollywood?"

"I didn't want to. My mother did."

"How old are you?" asked the Vermontster.

"I'm ten," Della answered.

"I'm fourteen. So Della, have you slept with any of the locals yet?"

A year and a half later, I would walk around a corner on the campus of Della's private school in Switzerland and catch her smoking marijuana.

Della wasn't twelve years old yet.

I remember the horrified look on Della's face when she saw me. I know I looked equally as horrified. I was dumbfounded at both Della's smoking marijuana *and* the sight of her scuzzy, angry-looking friends. Another one of God's photos that pops right out of His camera and into my brain.

But I'm getting ahead of myself.

It was Parents' Day at Della's school. I promised Della I would *try* to come from Los Angeles and visit her on Parents' Day. I had still never actually been to Della's school. Della didn't believe me when I said I might be coming. She had good reason not to. I had promised her many times before but usually changed my mind at the last minute. I was very busy in Los Angeles. I had five game shows on network daytime television Monday through Friday, and two at night, for a total of seven shows. I know Della would have been disappointed if neither her mother nor I showed up, but I was *really* busy. And I think at the time Parents' Day rolled around, Della's mother was off sailing somewhere in the Mediterranean.

Della, her roommate, and two other girls woke up very early

on Parents' Day morning to meet and smoke some pot before their parents arrived. The four of them had planned to do that for days. The two other girls were both thirteen, French, and roommates. Their room was down the hall from Della and the Vermontster's. The four girls were standing in a narrow alleyway between the chapel and the maintenance buildings. The girls were smoking marijuana to make them mellow enough to tolerate their visiting parents. Della didn't need pot to tolerate either her mother or me. The problem was, the girls had insisted Della take a few tokes, or so she said. My daughter habitually succumbed to peer pressure, never indicating to anyone that she had a mind of her own. Della checked her wristwatch, figured I wasn't coming, and began pulling on the doobie. That's when I walked around the corner of the building and saw her.

I saw four girls—the weird Vermontster on her one short crutch, two bedraggled and filthy little Frog harridans looking mean and cornered, and Della—frozen like deer caught in a car's headlights, all of them smoking marijuana. Della looked as tough as the other three, the girls daring any authority figure to take them on.

Much later I told Della, "The two French girls looked as though they just rolled out of bed and into the alley without brushing their teeth, washing their hands and faces, or combing their hair. They had dirt in the corners of their eyes and under their fingernails. I don't think either one of them had changed their clothes in weeks."

"But Daddy, they're French."

The Vermontster had lost one of her crutches. How does one lose a crutch? The Vermontster managed to do it. From what Della told me, and from what I could see, the girl was more bent over than before, and her bad leg—the one with the cast—was pulled back as if she were going to kick a soccer ball. The Vermontster looked like a featherless ostrich.

As I said, I looked just as bewildered as Della when we first saw each other. The entire scene was lethal. I was shocked and frightened. Panic-stricken. What should I do about it? Should I report the foursome to the school, including my daughter? Should I report the matter to the police? What? I had no idea.

So I did nothing.

And here's the really scary part. I looked at those four girls and suddenly I knew what my future with my daughter was going to be like.

4

It was March 1973. Della was eleven years old. Della would have told the story this way:

"It was exactly two in the morning by the electric clock next to my bed when I woke up from a sound sleep. It was a strange clock with strange numbers that shone in the dark and a strange bedroom. And then I remembered where I was. I was in London at the Dorchester. My mother and I had returned to Geneva from Los Angeles and I was back at the *école*. My father had come to Switzerland to take me to London for my Easter vacation. My father was sleeping in another room of our two-bedroom suite. I woke up because I was starved. We had eaten dinner that night at Mr. Chow and you know what they say about Chinese food.

"I remembered a package of cookies on top of the bar in the living room of our suite. They were Oreos. I wanted a couple. I got out of bed and headed for the living room. I tiptoed across the small hallway, past my father's bedroom door. I stopped and listened to hear if he was snoring. He wasn't, so I continued into the living room. The living room was lit up like a night baseball game. I know we didn't pay for electricity in the hotel, but still every single light was on. I thought that was strange. I was crossing the living room to the bar when I heard my father's voice say, 'Hello, Della.' I turned in the direction Daddy's voice was coming from. I could only see the top of his head. He was wearing sunglasses. Daddy was hiding behind the living room couch. Or trying to.

"'What are you doing, Daddy?' I asked, a tiny bit scared.

"'I'm drunk,' you said, holding up a half-empty bottle of scotch.

"'Why are you drunk, Daddy?'

"'Because I'm having a nervous breakdown. It's always good to be drunk when you're having a nervous breakdown.'

"'Why are you having a nervous breakdown, Daddy?'

"'Because I have to babysit *you* all the time. At least when I take you on vacations and because babysitting you gives me too many hours to think. And you know what I think? I think, What's to become of me? Where am I heading? What am I doing? Am I doing the right thing? I think truisms. I think maybe I should quit television. I think what the hell am I doing with my life anyway?'

"'But Daddy, your audiences love your shows. And they love you for creating them.'

"'Who said so? The public can't stand me *or* my shows. The public hates me. Have you ever read what the TV critics say about me?'

"'But you always said nobody pays attention to TV critics.

They criticize stuff that's *free*. You've always said TV critics, like the dinosaur, will someday be extinct.'

"'That's true. Did I tell you about the lady who called me over to the bar at the Palm restaurant?'

"'Yes you did, Daddy.'

"'You know the Palm restaurant? It's the place where you choked on that big hunk of meat and I had to give you the Hemlock maneuver.'

"'Heimlich.'

"'You know that story?'

"'Yes. The goddamned lady—'

"'Watch your mouth, Della.'

"'That's what you always say, Daddy. You always say, 'The goddamn lady at the Palm called me over to the bar but didn't compliment me like people usually did. This lady said I should be ashamed of myself for making up those stupid game shows.' Then you always say, "Jesus, Mary, and Joseph."'

"'That's what I say?'

"'Yes.'

"'Did I tell you about the other one? The fat slob of a woman who stopped me on Little Santa Monica?'

"'Yes. She told you you were using too many blacks on your shows. You told me about her too. Television's not what's bothering you, Daddy.'

"'It's not?'

"'No.'

"'You're right, television's not what's bothering me. It's just *part* of what's bothering me but not the whole thing.'

"'Then what's the whole thing?'

"'You. You're the other part of the whole thing.'

"'*Me?*'

"'I shouldn't tell you this but I'm going to anyway. You go to bed at nine o'clock at night, then I sit in this hotel room from nine until God knows when drinking scotch and staring at the ceiling. Eventually I go bonkers, get drunk, and think truisms.'

"'What's a truism, Daddy?'

"'Truths. Little horror stories. Like me thinking about all the hours of my life I'm wasting sitting in hotel rooms during *your* school vacations.'

"'Why do you make me go to bed at nine o'clock, Daddy? I could keep you company. We could play gin rummy and—'

"'You go to sleep at nine o'clock because you're young. You need your sleep. How old *are* you?'

"'Eleven going on twelve.'

"'Haven't you been eleven going on twelve for a long time?'

"'Seems that way.'

"'I'm sure you can stay up later than I let you. You think you can?'

"'Oh Daddy, sure I can. I stay up past midnight at school. When I'm at home, Mom doesn't care when I go to sleep. You're the only one who makes me go to bed early. Why do you make me go to sleep at nine o'clock?'

"'I don't know. Maybe to get rid of you so I can think.'

"'But I don't sleep and you don't think. You just said so yourself. You just hang around the suite drinking and popping out your little nightmares and having your little nervous breakdowns.'

"'So what?' you said angrily. 'I'm stuck in this damn hotel room staring at the four walls every night for three solid weeks.

You know in a given year I see you more than your mother does, if you count your holidays and summer vaca—'

"'I don't know what to tell you, Daddy. Daddy, why are you wearing sunglasses?'

"'The lights are too bright."

I never did get a sitter. But I didn't stay in the hotel room anymore either. I took Della out with me at night. I have this photograph the doorman took of the two of us standing in front of the Dorchester, about to go on the prowl. Della has her hair pulled back, showing off her very large forehead. She's wearing a red sweater under a double-breasted houndstooth overcoat. Her hands are in her pockets and she's leaning against me. She has a weird expression on her face. Sort of a smile, but not really.

I'm wearing a blue oxford button-down dress shirt, a dark blue and white striped tie, and a dark blue suit. I'm also wearing a brown overcoat with a red plastic American Legion flower in the overcoat's buttonhole that's been there for over a year. I too have a very strange expression on my face, though I'm not sure why.

Sometimes the two of us would go to a jazz joint and listen to music. Even though Della was a minor, I would get her into the club. We'd stand in the corner, me with a scotch and soda, and Della would drink a Shirley Temple. Sometimes we'd try and get into a gambling club, but Della wouldn't be allowed in no matter how much I begged. Sometimes we'd have a late dinner. We had fun in London, until Della got lost.

The two of us were walking in Hyde Park. It was a beauti-

ful day and Della was trying to convince me to rent a rowboat
so we could paddle hither and yon on the mini lake Londoners
called the Serpentine. I said we couldn't do that because Della
would end up doing something stupid like falling in and ruining
our entire day. As it turned out Della *did* do something stupid
that did sort of ruin the entire day. Well, if she didn't ruin it she
sure as hell put a dent in it.

We had gone to a restaurant in Hyde Park to have lunch. The
restaurant was built in a perfectly round circle, with six or seven
exit doors that sent you off in as many different directions. Della
got up to go to the bathroom, and when she came back she didn't
see me. I was at the counter getting another cup of coffee. So
Della went out one of the doors to look for me. That was dumb.
I mean *really* dumb. She should have just gone back to our table
and waited. She knew (or I thought she did) I wouldn't leave
the restaurant without her. When I got back to our table, Della
wasn't there. She wasn't in the ladies' room either. I asked. She
wasn't in the entire restaurant.

I, of course, panicked. I took off from one of the other doors.
Della and I were going in opposite directions in Hyde Park.
Hyde Park: a huge park to get lost in. I was convinced I was
never going to see my child again. Or that a pervert had grabbed
Della. Or that she had been kidnapped. Something horrible like
that. I always figured Della's mother would lose her someday,
but not me, not on my watch. And now Della's mother would
never let me forget it.

I ran this way and that. I stopped a policeman and asked if he
had seen a little girl, age eleven going on twelve, with blond hair
and a sort of longish nose, walking around anywhere? When
the policeman pulled out his notebook, I took off again. I didn't

have time to wait while the bobby took notes. And that's the way it was for about ten minutes, which seemed like ten hours. I was getting more frightened with each passing minute and figured the smartest thing to do was find the restaurant, go inside, and hope and pray Della would return. That's what I did. Della did the same thing. When I saw her I went bananas. Absolutely bananas.

I grabbed Della and kissed her all over her face.

Then I began screaming at her: "Don't you ever do something like that again! Do you hear? Don't you ever leave a place without me! Do you hear? Do. You. Hear?"

All the time I was screaming at Della I was pounding the center of her head with my forefinger. Stretched to its limit, my forefinger is unbending and hard as a nail. It's a wonder I didn't push a hole right through my daughter's skull and into her brain. A crowd stood in a circle around the two of us. It must have been interesting to watch me pound a hole in my daughter's head.

Unfortunately I couldn't take a picture. I was too busy at the time. But God took it. It's one of His best.

"One student smells bad all the time. Another, a girl, blushes bright red from head to toe at the mention of her name. And another, a tall bony guy, wears the same black slacks, white shirt, and black clip-on bow tie to school every single day and picks his nose constantly. Then examines it."

Della was talking about her new classmates at the grammar school in Malibu.

There's one snapshot I took of Della standing at the end of

a long line of students waiting to go inside the school building and start the day. Her blond hair is in a long pigtail hanging down her back. She's wearing a gray windbreaker over a
"stupid dress" (her words). None of the other kids are looking
at Della. None of the girls are in dresses. They're all in jeans
and T-shirts. Della didn't arrive with any jeans or T-shirts.
I was going to have to buy her some. It appears the students
are all giving Della "the silent treatment." (Her words.) None
of them know Della. None of them *want* to know Della. (Her
opinion.)

Della and I were miserable that day. "They only know that
I'm the 'new kid,'" she told me, using her fingers to make air
quotes. "And once again it's the middle of a school year. It's really terrible going to a new school as often as I do in the middle
of the school year. I'm just twelve years old and I've already
been to three different schools." She counted, using her little
fingers as numbers. "Montessori, the *école,* and now this Malibu
school."

I shrugged my shoulders and said, "It's only temporary."

"It doesn't matter," Della said. "It's still awful. Maybe it
wouldn't have been so awful if I had *started* here. But coming to
a school in the middle of the year makes me an outsider. Even if
it's for a little while. I'm always the outsider, the oddball. The
only place I wasn't an oddball was at Montessori, and you guys
pulled me out of there before I even got started."

"I didn't pull you out," I said.

"Oh yes you did," said Della. We were walking back from
school to my beach house. "If you didn't leave home I would
still be going to Montessori, wouldn't I?"

"I suppose so," I said.

"See?" she said. "And why couldn't Mom just leave me at the *école*? It would have been better than this."

"I don't know," I said. "We'll ask her."

Della's mother had to have an operation. She wanted the operation done in Los Angeles at Cedars-Sinai Medical Center. She should have stayed in Switzerland. She was told by at least a dozen of her friends the doctors and the hospitals were better in Geneva than any of the hospitals in Los Angeles. Della's mother disagreed.

"No way!" she said. "I'll be damned if I'm going to allow a Swiss idiot to operate on me. Let the Swiss stick to their clocks. Give me an American surgeon."

Della's mother pulled Della out of the *école* and the two flew to Los Angeles. When my ex-wife arrived in Los Angeles, she gave me Della. I was living in a new house on a cliff overlooking the Pacific Ocean in Malibu. My ex-wife told me to enroll Della in a nearby school.

"Why did you bring Della?" I asked. "How long do you expect to stay in L.A.?"

"I'm not sure. Maybe a couple of weeks."

"If you're staying such a short time, why didn't you just leave Della in her boarding school?"

"Because my stay here could be longer. Besides, I want to keep an eye on Della. She needs me to keep an eye on her."

Della didn't say anything. She just took my hand, and we walked away. As it turned out, Della's mother stayed in California for close to two months. I never saw my ex-wife while she was there.

My home was a beautiful old wooden thing. Della's grammar school was just a few blocks away. I think Della would have loved living with me in Malibu if she hadn't hated the school as much as she did. Della said the kids who went there were the worst. She said she thought the misfits at the *école* were bad. According to her, the kids at the *école* were just a bunch of harmless junkies. But the kids at Malibu were mean and spiteful and dumb as dirt. She said the bullies at that school were really bullies, and the suck-ups were the worst she'd ever seen. Della told me no one there liked her. I didn't know what to do about it. It was the beginning of a zillion things I wouldn't know what to do about.

I said stupid things like, "It's your imagination, honey. They really do like you."

"They do not!" she yelled. "The kids hate me at that dumb-ass school."

"Calm down," I said.

"Maybe, I don't know, maybe it's because I'm not one of them and never will be," Della said. "I'll always be the outsider. That's what I've been ever since you and Mom got divorced, an outsider. It's horrible being an outsider and being the butt of stupid jokes all the time. The kids at that stupid school ridicule me the way they ridicule Leroy Kunkle's stink and Mimi Blair's blushing. Kids are cruel."

Whenever I look at the snapshot of Della, standing in line waiting to go inside the Malibu grammar school, her school bag slung over her shoulder and her blond hair hanging down her back, I feel so sorry for her.

5

By 1975, Richard Nixon had been impeached and had left the White House, and NBC-TV showed their new hit program, *The Gong Show*, on daytime *and* nighttime television. That same year, Della's mother tired of the expatriate life. The two moved back to New York. Della was twelve and in the seventh grade. My ex-wife bought an apartment in the Riverside neighborhood of New York City and placed Della in the Horace Mann School. It was a good school, but tough. The *école*, with all its faults, and it had a ton of those, was academically better than I thought: Della was accepted at Horace Mann and did well. She said she liked the school and that the students were much "healthier" there.

Her biggest problem was the usual one: making new friends. She was never good at that. I think that's because Della was painfully shy, made that way I'm sure from always changing and entering new schools late in the term, as she was doing once

again at Horace Mann. Della was extroverted and crazy with
the few friends she knew well. Those friends really liked her. I
never understood why all the other kids didn't. They never gave
Della a chance or were mean to her from the start. Maybe it was
something in Della's own attitude. Maybe she came to these new
schools with a major chip on her shoulder.

Della's mother was glad to be back in the States. She con-
tacted old friends she knew when she lived in New York with
me in the fifties. She met some of those friends in the afternoon and did whatever ladies did in the afternoon, and others
at night for drinks and dinner. Della said that when her mother
was asked by her friends why she had moved to Switzerland,
her mother would mutter something that didn't make any
sense at all. Della told me she thought her mother's original
reason about Nixon sounded so foolish now she was embarrassed to mention it.

During one of Della's summer vacations, she told me about
her new life in New York. I never figured out why Della was
always so brutally honest with me. Maybe she was pitting me
against her mother, and vice versa, telling me things I didn't
want to hear about her mother and her mother things she didn't
want to know about me. Della was clever enough and mean
enough to do that.

"I would go home after school and stay in my room messing
with things," she told me, years later. "But I got tired of that.
I needed to fill my time doing *something* or die of boredom. If
Mom wasn't home when I got back from school, and she usually
wasn't, I would leave the apartment and roam the streets until
it got dark. Soon roaming the streets became a bore too. It's not
a whole lot of fun walking up and down the Riverside section

of New York checking out the local drugstore, the newspaper stand, the joggers, and the dog walkers. Of course there was the Hudson River straight out our living room window, but you know how I feel about historic sights and scenery. You see the Hudson River once, and you've seen it.

"I needed to do something else," she told me, "besides watch dogs poop and barges go by. I began stealing money from Mom's handbag. I'd grab a twenty before I left for school and use it in the afternoon to go to see films. I'm sure Mom would have given me the money to see a movie, but it was more fun stealing it. I looked my age, which was thirteen, so I couldn't get into R-rated movies or buy anything illegal like cigarettes or beer. It didn't matter. Mom was a heavy smoker. I found all the cigarettes I needed in our apartment, and since Mom entertained at home quite a bit, there was plenty of alcohol in the living room bar.

"If Mom ever started complaining about the vanishing alcohol and cigarettes, which she did once in a while, I would blame it on the maid. My mother fired two of them because of me telling on them. Most of the maids couldn't speak or understand English very well. They were always terrified and mystified when my mother walked them to the door. The way I looked at it, it was them or me."

When Della was older and told me all of this, her stories made me furious. How could a mother let her child go unsupervised like that? How could she? How could Della's mother be so negligent? Couldn't she see what was going on right under her nose? But that's not the way it really was. Not completely. It was years later that I realized how duplicitous and deceitful Della was during that time in her life. I discovered what a habitual liar she was and how she had become a master at playing one parent against the other.

At the end of May 1975, Della flew to Malibu to live with me in my beach house for June, July, and August, over her summer vacation. Actually the house wasn't on a beach. It was on a cliff overlooking the beach and the ocean.

My Malibu house was so cozy it was pathetic. It was an old wooden structure on two acres of land on Cliffside Drive. The house was what real estate agents called a tear-down. It meant that when I bought the house I was expected to tear it down and build a newer, bigger, and more beautiful one in its place. I would never have done that. To me, my "tear-down" was absolutely perfect.

My den faced the ocean. A fireplace went through the den to the adjacent living room. There was a very large kitchen with a table and six chairs. I had a wine rack built into the wall behind the table and chairs. The wine rack was filled with cheap bottles of California wine. The rack crashed to the floor during its first major California earthquake. There were two inches of wine on the kitchen floor. Next to the kitchen was the master bedroom with a fireplace and a bathroom. Both my bedroom door and the house's front door opened onto the kitchen. It was a strange layout, but as far as I was concerned, it was heaven here on earth.

For the three summer months of every year Della lived with me. She slept on a big comfy couch in the living room. The couch was about as big as a single bed. Louise Zafina, whom we called Weezy, was my housekeeper. She watched over Della. Weezy's sister Judy Ducharme would come to the house and take care of Della too. Della and Judy got along the moment they met. But Judy never stayed over. There wasn't any place for her to sleep.

I built a corral and tack shed on the acre next door to my house. It had been one of my dreams to own a couple of horses and keep them on my property. It was also one of my more bizarre ideas since I knew nothing about horses, nor did I ever show any inclination toward wanting to know. Up until that time I had never even *ridden* a horse in my entire life. But that didn't stop me from buying two big horses and keeping them in my corral.

I hired a hippie whose name I forget to take care of my horses. The hippie was a skinny guy with long unruly hair and an unruly beard. It was rumored that my horse guy was a member of Charles Manson's gang of cutthroats who allegedly lived in the hills along the Malibu coastline. It might have been true, but I doubt it. My hippie horse guy was too nice and gentle to be a Manson gang member. But then what did I know?

"Mansonman [Della's name for our horse guy] knows more about horses than I do and I trust him," I'd say to quell horrified inquiries.

I liked Mansonman. So did Della. He got me all the hay I wanted, and all kinds of other goodies I needed for the horses. Della told me years later she'd slip Mansonman a ten or twenty she had taken out of my wallet and Mansonman would get her drugs.

"Good stuff too," she said. "It was a great arrangement. Robin Hoodish."

One day, when Della was out somewhere with Judy, I walked into my kitchen to get something out of the refrigerator and

found one of my horses standing there. The horse wasn't wearing a bridle. Someone must have accidentally left the corral gate
open. The door to my kitchen was usually open. The horse
came down the street from the corral, up our driveway, through
the open kitchen door, and into the house. The sight of the huge
beast in the kitchen scared the hell out of me. Being essentially a
city boy, the problem of a horse in a kitchen and how to get him
out was never something I'd had to worry about.

And then I remembered that horses liked apples. I grabbed
three or four apples from the kitchen fruit bowl and chopped
them up into small pieces. I pulled my T-shirt out of my sweat-
pants, made a sack, put the cut-up apples in the sack, and led the
horse out of my kitchen by giving him little pieces of apple. I did
that all the way up the driveway, out along the street, and into
my corral next door. I told that story a lot. Della got so bored
of hearing it that when I started telling the horse-in-the-kitchen
epic to other people, she'd leave the room.

During those early years in Malibu, my television production company grew and grew. Sometime during the late sixties
my business had become a public company. I wasn't sure at the
time what the advantages were of going public, only that I became busier and richer. I owned a Rolls-Royce *and* a Porsche
convertible. (In those days owning a Rolls-Royce and a Porsche
mattered to me.) I had a house in Malibu *and* a small house in
Hollywood on a curvy street off Doheny Drive called St. Ives
Drive. I used the house in Hollywood when I was too tired to
drive out to Malibu. Or, as Della would say, when I had one of
my "secret assassinations" I wanted to hide from her.

With my business booming, I was away from home a lot.
I would explain to Della I was doing dog and pony shows to

raise money to buy other companies. While I was away, Judy Ducharme took care of Della. Judy and Della would always sleep in my bed. Eventually I added an addition in the same run-down style as the rest of the house: a dining room and above it, a spare bedroom. The spare bedroom had twin beds. Judy and Della finally had a place to sleep of their own. Della didn't have to sleep on the couch anymore and loved sleeping in the same room with Judy. Also Judy Ducharme could live with us and take care of Della full-time during Della's summers in Malibu. They shared that bedroom every summer until I sold the beach house. Della looked upon Judy as her second mother. Judy thought of Della as the daughter she never had. They fought and argued and made up. They did all the things mothers and daughters do. Judy wasn't as bright as Della. My daughter could do drugs behind Judy's back she couldn't do with me. Della could get whacked out of her mind on drugs and Judy would just look perplexed and say ridiculous things like, "You're something else, Della."

The two would remain best friends for Della's short life.

When Della was thirteen years old, she arrived in Malibu for the summer to find Eva Raintree, my girlfriend, living in the Malibu house. Eva had moved in with me before the summer started. According to Della, her summers were ruined now. I had begun dreading Della's visits, and now my girlfriend was being blamed for ending all the wonderful times the two of us had at my house in Malibu. But Della had to get a grip. Our lives were simply moving on. She was getting older, and I was becoming lonely.

Della detested Eva on sight. She called her Eva Braun. Della never lost her distaste for her, or her ability to make Eva miserable, a skill she would deploy with all my girlfriends. Eva Raintree-Braun was, according to Della, ugly as mud and dumb as dirt. Actually Eva was very pretty and extremely intelligent.

It was the beginning of a long era of me yelling at my daughter behind my girlfriends' backs for not liking various traits of theirs. It was also the time when my young daughter would ruin dozens of my relationships. It was a terrible period of my life. I didn't know how to handle my daughter's insolence. It marked the beginning of our toughest times together.

One day, when Della made a face once too often at Eva Raintree, I dragged her away from the dinner table by her arm. Outside I told her to stop making a face every time Eva laughed. I explained that Eva laughed a lot because she had a good sense of humor.

"She doesn't laugh, she giggles. Her giggling drives me *crayzee*," complained Della.

"She laughs."

"She giggles. And I have more humor in my little pinkie, Daddy, than Braun has in her entire body."

"Her name is Raintree."

"I mean if she had a sense of humor, Daddy, she could be forgiven. But Braun has no sense of humor what-so-ever. I mean none."

Once again, I didn't know what to say or do.

According to Della, there seemed to be a new girl living in my house every time she arrived for her summer vacation, which was hardly true. Some of those so-scalled girlfriends Della was talking about were women who were working on projects with me. One was an editor of a book I was doing. Several were television producers from my company who stayed for a while working on new projects.

Della hated all of them.

Some of my girlfriends brought their bad habits to the Malibu house, which disgusted Della, and sometimes me. One of them always forgot to turn off lights. One always left the closet doors open. My closets had those little bulbs inside that went off when the door was shut. Della followed that girl around shutting the closet doors before the bulbs burned out. She really hated having to do that. I didn't make her do it. Della shut the closet doors so she could complain about it. One girlfriend was a big slob. She left her underwear all over the house. One night we all came to the dinner table and found the girl's dirty panties hanging from the chandelier over the dining room table.

The girl saw the panties, giggled, and said, "So *that's* where they got to."

It didn't take me long to figure out who had put them there.

There was the self-proclaimed interior decorator who moved the furniture around in my bedroom while I was at work. I couldn't believe my eyes when I came home that night and saw the havoc she had created. I sent her packing immediately, much to Della's delight.

The question that always bothered Della was why couldn't I see the bad traits in my girlfriends that she and Judy could see immediately? Why would I allow those women to mess up our delightful household for such a long time? Della thought it was because I hated to fight. I *did* hate to fight. But that wasn't the reason. The reason was, I was hard-pressed to end a rather good union.

My girlfriends dreaded Della's arrival as much as she dreaded theirs. They realized that if Della continued to complain about them they would eventually be sent away. If, however, Della showed them any affection, there was a good chance they might stay indefinitely. My girlfriends and I wanted to stay together. But Della wouldn't allow it, if she could help it.

Della wasn't a wishy-washy kid. She was a force to be reckoned with. It was always Della versus my girlfriends. There wasn't any peace treaty, no such thing as live and let live. It was a constant war. As a result, all my girlfriends tried their best to get on Della's good side. They would volunteer to fix Della's hair, go shopping with her, pick out the clothes she should buy, help her with her makeup. Some of them even bought Della presents. To a point, Della naturally played along.

When I would confront Della with her vicious blackmail, she would cry and carry on, yelling at me, "Everything was fine until you started moving your girlfriends into our house. Why did you do that? Before your girlfriends came I had you all to myself. Now I have to share you. We would do everything together. Now when we go to the movies, three of us go. When we go for ice cream, a girlfriend comes along. Same thing happens when we go to the pizza parlor. Always one of your girlfriends has to come along. *That's* what bothers me. Big time. Me, you, and your girlfriend. I used to love it when we bowled together, roller-skated together, and surfed together, took rides in your car together. Now we don't do anything together."

Then Della would pout for the rest of the day and night. Della started refusing to come to the dinner table. She would eat in her room with Judy. I didn't mind that for a while. At least it was peaceful at the dinner table. During those long meals we ate together, Della would sulk more than she was pleasant.

She would put on the most horrendous face when she sulked. If she wasn't sulking she was glaring or making rude remarks she hoped were overheard by my girlfriends.

Eva Raintree scared Della. That's because I really liked Eva Raintree. Della started thinking I might marry her. Her panic usually resulted in my being forced to perform my "I Am a Grown Man" speech. During those infamous summers, Della heard the "I Am a Grown Man" speech over and over again. By the time Della was sixteen she could recite the speech by heart.

I would start by saying, "Della, I am a grown man just as someday you will be a grown woman. I have to live my life the same as you will. I have certain needs. Just because someone, some woman, is living with me doesn't change my love for you. I like Eva. I *love* you. My love for you will never stop, or lessen. Eva is my friend. You are my *daughter*."

I made the same speech when Eva Raintree was history. I would just substitute the new girlfriend's name: Susan is my friend. You are my *daughter*. Molly is my friend. You are my *daughter*. I even lived for a while with a woman whose nickname was Pigeon. When I said, "Pigeon is my friend. You are my *daughter*," Della burst out laughing. Della said she couldn't help herself.

Della would listen to me when I gave my little speech with the most bored expression on her face she could muster. From time to time Della would roll her eyes or stare at the ceiling. Once she twiddled her thumbs.

"So what are you so worried about?" I would always end up asking her.

One night at dinner a brand-new girlfriend corrected something Della said. Whatever it was, it made Della angry. She told my new girlfriend to go fuck herself. I don't remember ever being so mad.

I yelled, "Della, leave the house immediately."

"No," snapped the new girlfriend. "We'll straighten this misunderstanding up between us. Why don't you get yourself some fresh air for a few minutes."

I heard my girlfriend say as I left the house, "I know you hate me, you spoiled little brat, but this war is going to stop right now." I liked what she said.

What I didn't hear was Della saying, "You're dead meat."

Della went up to her room.

When I returned to the dinner table I said, "How did it go?"

"Fine," said the girl. "Della's upstairs pouting. Let her pout."

That night at two o'clock in the morning Della walked into my bedroom. Della turned on the lamp next to my bed. My girlfriend and I woke with a start. Our two heads popped up from our pillows in tandem.

Della said, "I can't sleep. I'm too upset. Your girlfriend called me a little hook-nosed Jew bitch. She said, 'Don't you start giving *me* shit, you little hook-nosed Jew bitch.'"

Della turned off the lamp by my bed and went back to her room.

"I said no such thing," said my girlfriend. "I wouldn't say something as horrible as that to your daughter."

The girlfriend was gone the next day.

It was during one of Della's summers in Malibu that I had what I thought was a great idea: having Della introduce me on *The*

Gong Show. Della wasn't thrilled. She asked me if I was sure she should do that.

I thought I heard some fear in her voice, which I wrote off to stage fright. I said, "Don't be afraid. Just do it. You'll have fun."

"I'm not afraid," she replied.

In the beginning of the program, the show's model, Sivi Aberg, would say, "And now here's the star of the show . . . *Chuck Barris!*" After a while stars like Carol Burnett and Steve Martin would introduce me. Then waitresses from Nate 'n Al's Deli in Beverly Hills would shout, "And now here's the star of the show and our favorite customer . . . *Chuck Barris!*" Then Della started introducing me. She would say, "And now here's the star of the show . . . *my daddy!*"

There are two snapshots showing Della introducing me. In the first photograph, Della's wearing a cute long-sleeved white shirt with red vertical stripes and black slacks. The sleeves of her shirt are rolled halfway up her arms. She's holding the microphone, but in the picture her arm is covering her mouth and she's pointing somewhere to her left. She had just said, "my daddy." That was the good one. There was one good picture and one very bad picture.

The best part of introducing me was that it gave Della a chance to be with me and hang out in the studio with the show's staff and the network's crew on weekends when we taped the programs. At the time, we were all one big, happy family. Marge Reck and Jennifer Cobb. Ruthie Goldberg and my secretary Loretta. Vince Longo, Jimmy Commore, his mother Sally, Mike and Ellen Metzger (they met at the company and married), Al and Linda Michaels (the same), Milton DeLugg, who led the Band with a Thug, Father Ed, Arte Johnson, Jaye P. Morgan,

Jamie Farr, Murray Langston, who was the Unknown Comic, Gene Patton (Gene Gene the Dancing Machine), and the program's director, John Dorsey. Most of the best memories of my life come from working with those people.

But I'm certain the idea of Della introducing me on television wasn't one of my better ones. I think I became aware of the potential repercussions too late. Unfortunately Della must have been thinking the same thing in the second picture.

The second picture's a bummer. It was taken about a year later. In the second photograph Della looks miserable. It's easy to see from the snapshot she doesn't like what she's doing. She appears to be trying to imitate Jaye P. Morgan, whom she loved. She's dressed in a man's fire-engine-red fedora, a red scarf knotted at her neck, a silk shirt, and a man's blue double-breasted suit. Her hair is cut short. She has rouge on her cheeks and she's wearing bright red lipstick. She's standing offstage waiting to introduce me. Della looks ridiculous and miserable. How did I let the makeup and wardrobe people do that to her?

The snapshot catches Della off guard. She looks horribly sad, as if she's aware of some impending doom no one else can see.

She once said to me standing backstage, "I don't know why you make me introduce you. If I didn't tell you before, I'll tell you now. It isn't a good idea. It just isn't. Maybe it's what I'm told to say. Maybe it's the way I say it. Maybe it's the makeup and the hairdos that make me look special, or different, or spoiled, or something. Maybe these days kids my age are jealous of sons and daughters of stars parading around like big shots. I don't know."

"Then don't do it anymore."

"Thank you, Daddy. I won't."

A few years later I wrote, directed, and produced a film called *The Gong Show Movie*. Columbia Pictures, the company that financed the movie, had a screening to test the public's reaction to the film. The screening was at the University of Southern California. The auditorium was packed to overflowing with more than fifteen hundred people, mostly students. I was extremely excited that evening, hoping for a good reaction.

Suddenly there was Della introducing me on a video clip in the film.

The entire audience booed!

I couldn't believe my ears. Do you know how horrible it is to be booed? Do you have any idea what being booed does to your feelings, your confidence, your self-esteem? It was catastrophic for Della. She ran out of the theater, sat on the base of some campus statue, and sobbed. I went running out behind her. I didn't know what to say to Della or how to act. All I kept repeating was, "Why did they do that? Why did they do that?"

6

It was the end of October 1976. Della was almost fourteen years old and had a crush on every member of the Bay City Rollers. She and her mother squeezed each other's hand as they watched *Carrie* at the movies. "At least you're not as awful as Piper Laurie," Della told her mother as they walked out of the theater. Her mother repeated the compliment for years.

One day in early November, I came to New York and took Della to Serendipity, the best ice cream parlor in New York City. They make fantastic sundaes and ice cream sodas there, and other scrumptious concoctions.

"Why are we going to Serendipity, Daddy?"

"To celebrate something. A surprise."

A young hostess showed us to a small table for two.

Della was thrilled. She loved surprises and apparently thought this surprise was a charm bracelet she had been pestering me about for months. She even suggested different charms. The thought of the bracelet made her bubble with excitement.

"So," I said, trying to act calm about my surprise, "before I tell you what my surprise is, let's order something. What would you like to have?"

"Tell me?" said Della, the expression on her face changing drastically. I was going to *tell* her what her surprise was and not *show* her, or *give* her. Della looked crushed.

Ignoring her sulking face as best I could and acting just as cheerful as before, I said, "I know you like a chocolate ice cream soda with vanilla ice cream. Let's get that. We can split it . . . two straws, two spoons."

"I'd rather have a vanilla ice cream sundae with chocolate syrup and wet walnuts," Della said, trying to be as contrary as she could.

"Okay, let's get that too."

"No. I'd rather have a malted milkshake," Della said, doing her best to be difficult.

"Okay, let's get that too."

"And their foot-long hot dog," she said, starting to giggle.

"I like their egg creams," I said. "Let's get the foot-long hot dog, an egg cream, and . . . and a root beer float!"

"Okay," she said, attempting to imitate me, "let's get that too."

We both started laughing. I mean *really* laughing.

The waiter arrived and asked if we were ready to order.

I said, "We certainly are. We'll have a chocolate ice cream soda with vanilla ice cream, a sundae with vanilla ice cream, chocolate syrup, and wet walnuts, a chocolate malted milkshake with vanilla ice cream, one of your foot-long hot dogs, an egg cream, and a root beer float."

"And for the young lady?" asked the waiter.

I was drinking water when the waiter said that. I laughed a surprised laugh, forcing water to come flying out of my nose and mouth, making me cough. The waiter whacked my back while I sat in my chair choking.

When the waiter was gone, I decided to spring my surprise. I said, "Guess what?"

"What, Daddy?"

"I have just been told by a judge in New York that I have custody of you. You are my responsibility now and not your mother's."

Della looked horrified.

I was shocked, deflated, and surprised. I expected Della to throw her arms in the air and jump up and down with excitement and joy. I realized at that moment that I had just made one of the biggest mistakes of my life. I instantly understood the realities of the situation. I had decided in recent weeks that I wanted Della to live with me, and her mother had simply agreed. All of Della's horror stories were lies, meant to make me furious with Della's mother. She had been playing the two of us against each other all along, and the tactic had backfired on her. Della obviously didn't really want to leave her mother and New York.

"I thought you would be overjoyed," I said, losing my appetite.

"I *am,*" Della said but she wasn't. I could tell.

"All these years you've been telling me those terrible stories about your mother," I said. "Like how there was this big rainstorm with lots of thunder and lightning, and you went to your mother's room to get in bed with her, but she had a guy in bed with her, and your mother told you that you couldn't come into the room. You told her you were scared and she said, 'Then sleep in the hall.' And that's what you did, slept the rest of the night in the hall, on the floor, against her bedroom door. And the one about how one of her boyfriends . . . never mind. I bet if I checked all your stories out with your mother I'd find out you made them all up. You did, didn't you, Della?"

"No! Yes. Well . . . ," she said, suddenly trapped.

Playing one parent against the other had produced an unexpected and undesired outcome for her. Now she would have to change schools again, which she hated to do. Meet new kids, something she also detested. Della would also have to leave her mother whom, I'm sure she was amazed to realize, she loved desperately.

Silence fell on our dessert-packed little table at Serendipity. I kept thinking to myself, *What have you done? What have you done?* Della and I had both been done in by Della's lies.

"I'm excited, Daddy. I really am," she said, the disappointment clearly apparent in her voice. "I can't wait to come live with you in California," she said. "Honest. I'm just . . . just . . . *surprised.*"

If I had looked in a mirror at that exact instant and seen my face, it would have looked as though someone had just told me about a death in my family. I sighed and went on with the charade.

"Okay, Della, it's almost Thanksgiving. Do you want to come to Malibu during the Thanksgiving break, or if that doesn't give you enough time, then how about during the Christmas break?"

"How about if I stayed in New York until the end of this school year?"

"Until the end of the school year," I said, exasperated. The horrors never seemed to end.

"Yes. How about if I come in June? That way you'll have enough time to get ready for me, and I'll—"

"Okay, okay. June, June."

We finished our desserts in silence, pushing most of them away.

By the time Della arrived in California to stay with me as my responsibility, I had sold the Malibu house and was living full-time in the Hollywood Hills on St. Ives Drive. When Della asked me why I sold the Malibu house, I told her living by myself on a cliff overlooking the ocean was too lonely for me. I told her being near the ocean made me drink too much, especially on weekends around four o'clock in the afternoon when the sun started going down.

"What happened to all your girlfriends?" Della asked rather cheerfully. "Didn't you always have some girl around to keep you company?"

I shrugged my shoulders.

The Hollywood house on St. Ives Drive was a cute little upside-down affair. You could get to the front door of the house by going down some stone steps from the street. Or you could go through the garage. The garage was on top. There was a stairway from the garage that led downstairs to the kitchen. The kitchen, dining room, living room, Della's bedroom and bath, and a small powder room by the front door made up the first floor of the upside-down. Della told me that once in a while, she would go to sleep and wonder if a big earthquake would come

along and suddenly she'd end up sharing her bed with my red
Porsche Speedster convertible.

Della's bedroom in my upside-down house was actually
very cozy. Her bed was a big wooden four-poster. Della had all
her little "nernies" as she called them (stuffed animals) neatly
placed on the night table by her bed. Over on the bureau were
her special Christmas and birthday cards. At the foot of her bed
were her big stuffed animals. She had tons of them and knew
them all by name. On the mantel over the fireplace was her snow
globe collection. I would usually buy Della a snow globe when
I came home from a business trip. Della loved snow globes.
And her doll collection. Now and then, I would also bring her a
wonderful doll from a foreign country I had visited. The dolls
had beautiful silken clothes. Della named each one and talked to
them as if they were human.

The big stone fireplace in Della's bedroom was in working
order. On one side of it was a large bronze bucket filled with
logs. A bronze pail for kindling was on the other side. Her bedroom also had a very comfortable rocking chair and a big television console in a wooden cabinet. A thick green rug covered the
floor and there was green wallpaper on the walls. Della loved
her bedroom.

The living room had a second fireplace and windows that
overlooked the city of Los Angeles. There was a door that
led out to a small terrace. Once in a while, if the weather was
particularly good, Della and I ate breakfast or dinner on the
terrace.

Downstairs was the bottom floor. That's where my bedroom
and bath were. My bedroom had a fireplace, a large walk-in
closet, and a large bathroom with a great tub. I had a good-sized

office next to my bedroom with a door that led out to a small stone terrace and enclosed garden.

I brought my two dogs with me to Hollywood from the Malibu house. They were big dogs, too big for the little house, but I couldn't part with them. There was Goldie, a female purebred golden retriever, and a gray, white, and black English sheepdog mix I rescued one day from the pound. Della named him Rags.

When Goldie and Rags met, it was love at first sight. At night, the two dogs would lie on their stomachs side by side in front of the fireplace and Goldie would clean Rags's ears. The lady and the tramp. It was really sweet. Eventually Goldie became pregnant and gave birth to eleven of their puppies in my bedroom at the Malibu house.

Della's grandmother called while Goldie was having her puppies. She said to me, "Make sure Della's not around when the girl dog gives birth. It wouldn't be good for her to see the birth process, the afterbirth, all that ugly mess. It could traumatize her for life. She might never want to have a baby."

I explained to my mother that her call was too late. "Your granddaughter is sitting cross-legged on the bedroom floor right beside Goldie watching everything, the placenta, the afterbirth, everything, while eating a peanut butter and jelly sandwich."

My mother was a major-league anti-Semitic racist nut, despite being Jewish herself. When Della dated a boy from North Korea, my mother wouldn't allow the two of them to visit her.

"I'm not having any Chink in this apartment," my mother said to Della.

"He's not Chinese, Gran," Della tried to explain. "He's North Korean."

"Same thing."

Della dated a black guy too. My mother told Della, "If your grandfather knew his granddaughter was dating a nigger, he'd be twirling around in his grave."

"Jesus, Gran," said Della, "they only use the n-word in the South."

"What's the n-word?"

"Nigger."

"Well honey, I'm from the South. South Philly." My mother cackled.

"That's not funny, Gran."

"Didn't say it was. Get rid of the nigger."

Della once told me, "I never thought Jews were anti-Semitic. Or racists. I always thought Jews were the racees."

My mother was ninety-two when she died. The ancient racist kicked the bucket in her bed at home, pain free and peacefully. I guess racists have it made. It seems to me they live longer and die the sweet simple way. The good guys get assassinated: Martin Luther King, both Kennedys, Abraham Lincoln. John Lennon. The list goes on and on.

Anyway, we kept one of Rags and Goldie's pups. Della named him Boozer.

Della started at Westlake, a private all-girls school. In the snapshot I took on her first day, she's dressed in her school uniform, and Rags is sitting beside her. He's looking to his right. Something must have caught his eye. Della's looking at the camera. The two are in the living room of my house in the Hollywood Hills.

"Boy, you look cute!" I told her. Della rolled her eyes.

I decided to enroll Della in a private school, but not a boarding school. I wasn't going to make the same mistake Della's mother made in Switzerland. Westlake had an excellent reputation.

"Guess where the girl who was number one in her class at Westlake last year decided to go to college?" I asked Della one evening after reading a Westlake catalog.

"Where?"

"SMU," I said with an inordinate amount of excitement. I thought that was kind of terrific. Here was a young girl with good grades, probably could have gone to Harvard or Yale, and she decided to go to SMU.

"What's that?"

"What's what?"

"SMU?"

"Southern Methodist University!" I said. "And you know why she chose SMU?"

"Why?"

"Because her *father* graduated from there," I said contentedly.

"How 'bout them apples?" muttered Della.

"Do you know where you might want to go to college?" I asked.

"No."

"You do well at Westlake," I said, "and you'll be able to go anywhere."

The Westlake campus was beautiful. It looked like a small college. It had rolling lawns and beautiful woods surrounding the campus. It was academically tough. At that time, the Westlake School boasted that all of its seniors were accepted into the college of their choice. When I visited the school, I noticed that the students were normal and not misfits. That was good news.

The other good news was that Della's marks were good from her preparatory schools in Geneva and New York. She passed the Westlake entrance requirements. She would start at the beginning of a new school year and not in the middle.

The bad news, as far as Della was concerned, was (1) no boys, and (2) everyone had to wear a uniform. At the *école* there were boys (eventually), and at the Horace Mann School there were boys and no one had to wear uniforms. The students could dress any way they wanted to.

Westlake girls, in the lower grades, wore crisp white blouses and gray skirts. Navy blazers or navy sweaters were added on cold days. Seniors wore solid navy or navy and green tartan plaid skirts with white blouses and navy sweaters. In the spring and fall the girls wore powder blue cotton dresses buttoned down the front.

To be rebellious, some of the students walked around study hall with their dresses unbuttoned. Della became friends with a girl named Eustace—the two were pothead buddies I later found out—who unbuttoned her dress low all the time in study hall. Eventually she was caught and expelled—for the dress code violations, not the pot. That was really bad news for Della, because Eustace was really good at scoring grass.

Something about the Westlake School for Girls reminded Della of a convent. I, on the other hand, loved everything about the school: the fact that it was an all-girls school, the uniforms, the tough academics, everything.

I drove Della to school in the morning, which I enjoyed doing. The entrance to Westlake had a half-moon driveway that went up a hill to the school's front door, then down the hill back to the street. In the morning there was always a line of cars moving slowly toward the top. When we were close to the school's main entrance, Della would kiss me on the cheek. I always loved the kisses I got from Della in the morning as she got out of the car. She loved the smell of Lilac Vegetal, my aftershave lotion. When I finished shaving in the morning I would shake some of the Lilac Vegetal onto my hands, rub my hands together, and lightly slap the lotion on my cheeks. Then I'd rub a little bit on Della's nose. She always laughed when I did that. I loved Della's nose, which seemed to be getting more Semitic looking every day.

It wasn't long after Della started at Westlake that she began to loathe *everything* about the school. "Westlake's too hard," she said. "It's the toughest school I've ever been to. It's tougher than the *école* and Horace Mann put together."

Della seemed to be in a perpetual funk mostly because, along with the school being hard, she had tons of homework to do every night.

Della told me she was used to doing her homework when it was raining outside, or snowing, or just plain freezing, like it usually was in Switzerland and New York. "I don't like doing homework in California where the weather's warm and balmy all the time," she said. "And I have to wear that dumb uniform every day."

What I didn't know was that Della couldn't get her hands on any drugs at Westlake. The marijuana her friend Eustace provided went with Eustace when she was kicked out of school. Della's life suddenly lurched from goofing the day away on the high side to working her buns off. After about a month of

Westlake she started crying herself to sleep at night, or pretending to.

I would come to her room before she went to bed and ask her what the problem was, knowing exactly what the problem was.

"I hate Westlake, Daddy."

I would blink a few times, wondering what to say. I would end up saying, "I understand why you don't like it. It's another new school and that's hard for you. But it will get better and better. You'll see."

It was during these times I realized how much I needed a partner, someone who knew what to say in this type of situation, who could help me raise my daughter.

"It *won't* get better and better, Daddy," Della screamed. "It will get worse and worse. It's too hard."

I hated this. "Della, stop it. Keep your voice down. Don't yell at me. I'm not yelling at you. I'm *talking* to you. It will get better, Della. You'll see."

"I mean it's always sunny and . . . and . . . and there aren't any boys."

"No boys, huh? Well, there won't be any distractions. That's good. You'll be able to concentrate on your grades. You'll be able to go to any college you choose. You'll see."

"Stop saying, 'You'll see'!" Della shouted. "I *won't* see. I hate Westlake, Daddy. I want to go to a co-ed school. How would you like going to an all-*boys* school? Not very much, I'll bet."

Here Della added another spur-of-the-moment line. "I'm tired of hanging out with lesbos."

"With what?"

"With lesbians, Daddy. Westlake is overrun with lesbians."

"So what if there are lesbians?"

*   *   *

Roughly a month passed. Suddenly Della's report cards became atrocious.

One night I confronted her in her room. "Della, what happened to your grades? They're awful. Teachers are calling me to come to school for 'chats.' What's going on? What happened to you? I don't have time to go to your school for 'chats.' Not these days. I have too much to do in the office to go running to teachers' conferences every week. These are very busy times for me. Get a grip, Della."

"The school's way too hard, Daddy. And I . . . uh . . . I missed too much."

"You missed too much what?"

"Too much preparation . . . from the previous years."

"You did not."

"I *did*. And I can't stand the uniforms."

"I think the uniforms are cute."

"Westlake's awful, Daddy. It's full of lesbians. There aren't any boys. Just a school full of lesbos." Della had decided to heavy up on the lesbian issue.

There would be a time when I would look back and wish with all my heart that Della had become a lesbian, if being a lesbian would have provided her with a happy, healthy life.

"Westlake isn't fun anymore," Della ranted on. "Every other school I went to was fun. Even that dumb Malibu grammar school was more fun than Westlake."

"I thought you hated the Malibu school," I said, confused.

"It was more fun than dumb Westlake, Daddy. At least it had boys, not *lesbians*."

"What school would you rather go to?" I asked stupidly.

"Beverly Hills High School," she answered immediately.

"But we don't live in Beverly Hills."

A week later I rented an apartment on Charleville and South Rodeo Drive. I used the apartment as a hideout. Now Della had a Beverly Hills address and could go to Beverly Hills High School. That was my second biggest mistake, taking Della out of Westlake and putting her in Beverly. My *biggest* mistake was taking custody of her.

There would be more mistakes to come. Sending Della to Beverly Hills High was just the tip of the iceberg.

Drugs, dope, and alcohol were rampant at Beverly Hills High, especially for susceptible kids like Della. Della overdosed on too much cocaine and vodka a week after she started there.

Della overdosed for the first time when she was fourteen years old.

The last thing she remembered was passing out on someone's lawn.

Then she recalled slowly waking up and realizing she was in a strange bed, and that I was standing by her bed, and I was wearing a tuxedo.

Della said, "Hi, Daddy."

"Hi."

"You look cute, Daddy. I'm in a hospital, right?" It didn't take her long to figure *that* out.

I said, "How are you doing, sweetheart?" My eyes said, *Oh my God!*

"I'm doing okay."

"What happened, Della?"

"I was at a party, and I guess I drank too much alcohol. I never drank alcohol before."

"Did you take any drugs?"

"No, Daddy. I just drank too much vodka."

I smiled and asked again if she was okay.

"I guess so," she said, and managed a weak smile.

A female doctor came into the room. I remember that she was dressed in a white coat with a stethoscope around her neck. She wore a pin with her name printed on it—Dr. McGinty—and asked me who I was.

"I'm this girl's father."

"I see. How old is she?"

"Fourteen."

"Your daughter overdosed on cocaine and a lot of alcohol," said the doctor. "I'm not sure how many amphetamines and barbiturates she swallowed. I'll tell you this, you're lucky your daughter's alive. We pumped her stomach as soon as she got here. We got rid of all the poisons. Just in time, I might add."

I said nothing. Nor did Della, lying in the bed behind us.

The doctor continued: "I understand someone at the party your daughter was attending tried to find you or your wife for quite a while. The person who phoned the hospital said your daughter was lying unconscious outside on the lawn for a long time. Thank goodness someone called an ambulance, and not a moment too soon. Neither you nor your wife could be found. Is that true?"

"Well . . . I . . . uh . . . I was at a black-tie affair," I said, "one of those industry things. I'm not in the habit of leaving a forwarding address, and as far as my wi—"

"It's a good thing that someone called an ambulance when he or she did," the doctor said. "As I said, if that person had waited much longer your child would have died. Why is a young girl like your daughter allowed to attend parties where drugs and alcohol are prevalent?"

"Is that any of your business?" I asked angrily. Why was she yelling at me? I wasn't the one who took the drugs. "Shouldn't you be telling me my daughter's medical condition and not lecturing me about parental care?"

"You're right," she said. "I most definitely should *not* be lecturing you. But I see so many of these young children ingesting so many drugs and so much alcohol in Beverly Hills, it's starting to drive me nuts. Off the record, just between you and me, shouldn't you be putting your foot down? Shouldn't you and your wife be stricter about what your daughter does and where she goes at her age?"

"One of my problems is that I don't have a wife. I wish I did. I could use the help."

"Then you have a double burden." The doctor was unfazed by my excuse. "You *must* be aware how dangerous this whole drug problem is these days. You are, aren't you?"

The doctor continued, "Most children your daughter's age don't know a thing, don't have a clue about what they're getting into or how to protect themselves. Nor do they know how to stand up to peer pressure. Very few kids between the ages of thirteen and sixteen have minds of their own."

"So what do you propose I do, particularly as a single parent?"

"Talk to her. Don't yell at her. Hug her. Give her a lot of affection. Talk to her with kindness and understanding and *keep* talking to her. Talk to her over and over again. This is your biggest job right now, the biggest job of your life. *You* have to train your daughter to be aware of the dangers of drugs and alcohol. You *must* talk to her until you're blue in the face. If she fights you, persevere. You've got to keep talking until you think—no, until you *know*—she understands. You'll know it when she does. It's your obligation to keep a tight rein on your daughter, to be supportive, open, and talkative during these dangerous years, during her early teens. Children must be taught, they must be lectured to. They've got to know it's *not* embarrassing to say no to drugs and alcohol. And cigarettes too. Children are like puppies, Mr.—"

"Barris."

"Children are like puppies, Mr. Barris. Children must be trained not to succumb to peer pressure, particularly when it comes to drugs, just as puppies must be trained to be housebroken."

"Will this . . . this talking to my daughter work?"

"Yes. If you persevere. This is the time you *must* be tough, Mr. Barris. Really tough. These are the critical years."

I stood there feeling embarrassed by the doctor's long reprimand.

"My daughter's overdose tonight is going to be my wake-up call. And hers."

She had heard that junk before, a thousand times. The doctor had experienced fathers like me, and mothers too, more times than she'd like to remember. Rich talkers, full of themselves, full of excuses and platitudes. Especially in Beverly Hills. Always racing to the hospital from some black-tie function, all wide-eyed and panic-stricken, all spouting the same nonsense, over and over again: *My daughter's overdose tonight is going to be my wake-up call.*

When I asked if I could take Della home, the doctor didn't answer. Instead, she turned around and asked Della how she felt.

Della said, "I feel good."

"Then I'll tell the nurse to get your clothes," said the doctor, "and you can go."

"Really?" Della said, hoping the doctor didn't hear the disappointment in her voice.

A nurse brought Della's clothes and pulled a green curtain around her bed. The nurse helped her get dressed. I took Della home.

7

I have this vivid snapshot in my mind, a photo God took, of Della, my new girlfriend, and me sitting at the dinner table in our Hollywood house. God took the picture the moment I slapped the dinner table so hard the water sloshed onto the table from the water glasses. My face was beet red as I yelled, *"We'll do it tonight."*

Let me back up a little.

When Della went back to school the week after she overdosed, she was startled to find that she was *not* the topic of conversation at all. In fact she was anything but. She was shunned more than ever. Della had become a heroine to some of the school's losers but a loser to the majority of the school's students. Being a druggie wasn't like being a cheerleader, or an honor student, or the captain of the field hockey team. So in effect nothing changed, except Della had a new nickname. OD, or Odee. It was used by boys, mostly.

"Here comes Odee. Let's change the subject to drugs."

"What are ya snortin' this morning, Odee? What's the drug of choice among the addicts?"

"Hey, Odee. Can I check your eyeballs?"

If Della had any plans of joining the established cliques of popular girls before, she was out of luck for good and always. She had become an instant outcast, a troublemaker, a doper.

Many years later, sitting on a bench in Beverly Glen Park, Della said to me, "Maybe my problem was simply me being me. When I went to the Montessori school I had tons of friends. But that was then. I think when you guys got divorced, your divorce changed me. And then when I left the Montessori school I changed some more. And then when I went from school to school I changed some more. I became angry. I carried a permanent chip on my shoulder. Maybe if you and Mom stayed together and I had stayed in the States and I had gone to the same schools with the rest of my friends I would have been a damned cheerleader and ended up going to a great college. Who knows? I *do* know becoming a druggie certainly wasn't the answer," said Della. "Not that I was going to stop being a druggie. The highs were too good. That's the trouble with drugs. You become addicted.

"And because of drugs, all I got from my fellow students at Beverly was a perpetual cold shoulder. I was warned to stay away in no uncertain terms. You know, the way kids warn one another to stay away from their lunch tables, their street-corner gatherings after school, and their weekend parties. I was banished from everything. Being banished by the popular kids at Beverly Hills High pushed me right into associating with the lowlifes and misfits who loitered in the streets and back alleys near school. Kids who didn't make the teams, didn't make the great cliques, didn't sit at the great lunch tables, and weren't invited to anyone's parties. My new friends were not the nice kids who made up the bulk of the student body. What I was left with were the dorky guys, the dimwits, the ones who were flunking their courses, the tattooed and leather-jacketed toughs, the disliked and the shunned. When I look back on my life, I think overdosing during my first week at Beverly was the crusher, the one thing, the one event that changed my life the most."

Della became queen of the outcasts. She stopped doing her homework and spent her nights roaming the streets with other low-life friends getting stoned out of their minds. When she came home at some ungodly hour, I would check her pupils. They were always dilated, and I would have a fit. I forbade her to be out so late, but she ignored me, and I didn't do anything about it. I never punished her. When I did, she'd just ignore it. I felt helpless. What was I to do, lock her in her room?

I had forgotten all about how I felt in the hospital room with Della, and did almost nothing to change myself or Della before things got any worse. Della began to disobey me more and more. She stayed out late against my instructions. Sometimes she didn't come home until early morning. Sometimes she didn't come home at all. I began receiving phone calls that woke me from a sound sleep. Horror calls, I called them. My telephone would ring at twelve, one, two in the morning. Each phone call revealed a new and frightening situation Della had gotten herself into. Though she didn't have a driver's license, she would take my car keys and my car and get into accidents until I hid the keys. The telephone would ring at some wee hour of the morning and it would be Della mumbling something about hitting someone's car and would I come and get her.

Neighbors would complain of Della being drunk and disorderly on their lawns and I would have to leave my bed and bring her home. The more of those horror calls that came in at night, the more lost and panic-stricken I felt. The more Della ratcheted up the nightmare phone calls, the more nervous and helpless I became. On more than one occasion Della was arrested in various department stores for shoplifting. Once, at the Saks Fifth Avenue store on Wilshire Boulevard, Della was arrested for shoplifting more than fifteen hundred dollars' worth of merchandise. I would have to leave the office at the worst possible time (her calls always came at the worst possible times). I would talk myself blue in the face on Della's behalf, which usually meant nothing. I would invariably end up paying for the stolen merchandise so the criminal charges would be dropped. Every morning I woke wondering what sort of nightmare was in store for me that day. And still, Della didn't forget to make my girlfriends' lives miserable.

I tried sending Della to rehab centers, but she refused to go. I begged Della to see a doctor, go to a psychiatrist, join an intervention group, but she wouldn't do anything I told her to do. Once I tricked her into driving with me to Palm Springs for two days of sun and fun. Della was suspicious. When we got to Palm Springs, I handed Della over to a detox center and drove away. Della ran away from the center the next morning, thumbed a ride back to Beverly Hills, scored some drugs, got smashed, and came home that night. I already knew Della had run away from the detox center. The center had telephoned me. When Della walked in the door, I looked worse than she did.

Della joined a gang of roughnecks. They were all school truants, dropouts, druggies, and bullies. They would grab boys and girls walking home after school and rob them of whatever money they had in their wallets and anything else valuable. They bullied them into not saying anything to their parents. They would surround goody-goody girls traveling in groups of three or fewer and take their money. The more successful Della's gang became the more other toughs wanted to join.

Della was the gang's leader. She wasn't afraid to swallow whatever drugs were around. She had the dirtiest mouth. She was the one who did the punching and slapping. She had found a home, of sorts.

One night Della decided to come home in time for dinner. I was already troubled that Della was never around the house for meals. The problem was, I didn't know what to do about it. Also, I didn't want to lose the newfound peace and quiet at the dinner table. It was a delightful break from constantly yelling and shouting at my daughter.

The night I was talking about, we were all sitting at the dinner table: me, my new girlfriend, a tall, thin young lady with a beautiful face named Betty Ketterer, and Della. The phone rang. I got scared. I don't know why I did, I just did. I guess it was a Pavlovian reaction. Phones scared me. (Late-night phone calls still do.) Weezy answered the phone in the hallway. She said it was for me and waited until I walked to the hall to hand me the phone. Silence had struck the dinner table. All three—Della, my girlfriend, and Weezy—listened to my end of the telephone conversation.

"Yes, this is Mr. Barris. Yes . . . yes . . . uh huh . . . I see . . . When? Uh-huh. And . . . and how badly is she hurt? Uh huh . . . She had to go to the hospital? That's terrible. I'm so sorr—uh huh . . . What was taken? I'm sorry, I couldn't hear—her wallet? You did? I see . . . Well, rest assured I will make absolutely certain everything is returned. Yes. Of course . . . I will pay the hospital bill. What was the hospi—uh huh . . . What did your daughter say? It has happened before, has it? Yes . . . It's happened to others, you say . . . I will—I certainly will. I'll make absolutely sure it will *never* happen again, to anyone. I appreciate your calling. Yes . . . and . . . and I appreciate your not reporting this to the police or the school authorities. Yes—this time—I understand. Thank you again . . . and . . . pardon? Yes . . . yes I will . . . I'll be over tonight with your daughter's things and your money. Good-bye."

I returned to the dinner table white-faced.

The beautiful girl named Betty Ketterer asked what had happened.

"Apparently," I said, "Della is the leader of a gang of toughs who have been robbing their schoolmates. Della's gang trapped this girl, the one whose mother just called, and roughed her up. Badly, I might add. The girl's mother said Della punched her daughter in the chest, opened her backpack, dumped everything onto the pavement, and Della's gang took whatever they wanted, which in this case amounted to the girl's money, a new wallet, and a bracelet. Then Della apparently slapped the girl again, this time hard, across the girl's face. The smack opened the girl's bottom lip. Della warned the girl not to say a word about it or they would all, in Della's words, 'come back and beat the crap out of you.' The girl told her parents, anyway. The girl's parents took her to the emergency ward of Beverwil Hospital because the girl was dizzy and out of sorts from the punch in the chest Della gave her. The parents wanted all of her things back including the girl's money *and* her hospital expenses, which I think is very fair. They could have sued me for zillions or reported everything to the police and the school authorities."

I paused to take a deep breath. I was embarrassed that all this was happening in front of my new girlfriend.

"Tonight," I said, "I will drive Della over to the girl's house—"

"No, Daddy, not tonight. Tomor—"

"We'll do it tonight." I had never raised my voice to Della like that before, with such anger and violence. Della said, as we sat on our bench several years later, she would never forget the terrible expression I had on my face. It was an unforgettable memory embedded on both our brains forever. One of God's photos.

"And you will be grounded for a damn month," I fumed. "You will stay in your room after school for an entire month, if I have to stand outside your bedroom door myself. Do you hear?"

"Yes I hear, Daddy," Della whispered.

There was a deathly silence at the dinner table. And then I said, "Della, you're a walking nightmare!"

A walking nightmare. I had called my daughter a walking nightmare in front of other people.

That night Della and I took everything my daughter had

taken from the girl, her wallet and her "tacky bracelet" (Della's angry words), to the girl's house. Della didn't have all the stolen money. When I asked why not, she said it was divvied up among those who had done the robbery. She told me how much they had taken and I made up the difference, along with money for the girl's hospital bill.

Della apologized to the girl. Della also apologized to her parents. She lowered her eyes and appeared extremely sorrowful. She could look extremely sorrowful if she put her mind to it. None of the family cared how sorrowful Della looked, especially the girl. Her lip was still swollen and black and blue. Della and I were not invited into the house. The entire family stood in the doorway: the girl, her father and mother, and her older brother. Everyone in the family hated Della. You could feel it.

The girl's brother said to Della, "If you or your gang ever lay a finger on my little sister again I will personally break *your* forehead, Della."

I remember being so mortified standing there that I didn't say a word in Della's defense. Della told me during the ride home, "I was pretty good, wasn't I, Daddy? I was doing really good remorse. Maybe I'll become an actress."

I told her to be quiet.

The first two weeks of Della's grounding I picked her up at school and drove her home. I never spoke to her. I made sure Della was in her room. I stayed in the living room working on something. During the third week I went back to my office. I had Weezy pick up Della at school in a cab and take Della straight home. I called several times in the afternoon and asked to speak to Della. I had nothing to say to her. I just wanted to make sure she was at home. During the fourth week when I called to check up on Della, Weezy always said she was in her room. Weezy never told me the truth, and I never asked to speak to Della.

Della knew by the fourth week that I was back to not really wanting to know what she was doing. Della called me Mr. Ostrich Man. "Better he sticks his head in the sand than knows what his daughter's doing. That's Mr. Ostrich Man's motto," she told her friends.

8

It was December 24, 1978, Della's sweet sixteenth birthday. During these years there was always a peace treaty struck around Della's birthday that lasted through the Christmas holiday.

Della always said all kids born on December 24 got the short end of the stick. She was referring to birthday and Christmas presents. My guilt-stricken soul always went overboard on those two occasions. I would buy Della two dozen presents to cover both days. The "Christmas girlfriend," as Della called her, and I waited with bated breath while Della opened one magnificent gift after another.

"Daddy, you really didn't need to buy me so many presents. And anyway, I'm turning over a new leaf, starting today."

"It's your sweet sixteen birthday, honey," I said. "It's a big one."

"Your daddy says you always say you're turning over a new leaf today," said my girlfriend.

"Who asked you?" said Della.

"Easy, Della," I said.

"But what about Christmas, Chuck?" asked my girlfriend, apparently unfazed by Della. "Christmas is tomorrow."

"I have more presents for tomorrow," I said.

"Oh God, you *do?*"

My new girlfriend's name was Margarita. One name. She had a last name, but she wanted to be called just Margarita. Margarita figured she was destined for greatness. She was going to be either a wonderful actress or a wonderful singer. "Something in 'the Biz,'" as she liked to say. Margarita was convinced the one name would do the trick. I couldn't quite understand what she meant by her saying her name "would do the trick." What about talent? I decided not to pursue it. But Della did.

"So what if you don't make it in 'the Biz'?" Della had asked.

"I'll be a nurse," Margarita answered.

Margarita was chubby, with a great face, blond hair, and a cute but plump figure. And she was funny. I think she would have made a great comedian.

Della had whispered to me behind Margarita's back, "You know she'll be fat as a blimp someday."

"Don't start."

Della's birthday presents (so far) included a cashmere sweater, a great-looking raincoat that belted in the front, three different scarves (in one box), a pair of fur-lined gloves, and five hundred-dollar gift certificates from five trendy stores. The gift certificates were wrapped in huge boxes to trick Della. But . . . until now no gold Rolex ladies' bracelet wristwatch, the present Della *really* wanted, and had been yearning for, and hinting about for months.

Della had told me weeks and weeks before about how all the hotshot girls at Beverly Hills High School had gold Rolex bracelet wristwatches.

I said, "Really?"

And though I knew Della despised Beverly Hills High School girls because they had all snubbed her, she coveted the gold Rolex watches they all wore. Della described in great detail why she wanted the watch. She said, "I mean, the way I figure, if I can't hang with those hotshot girls, at least I can wear the watch they all have. I can just see myself strutting through the halls flashing my gold Rolex bracelet watch in their faces, Daddy, with a look on mine that says, *So there, rich bitch, you're not so hot after all, are you? Look at me. I've got a gold Rolex bracelet wristwatch too.*"

In any case, the Rolex hadn't made an appearance yet, and just two wrapped presents remained to be opened. I could see that Della kept trying to judge the size of the two boxes, ever hopeful, wondering where it was. She knew if I had bought the watch I would try to fool her. I would have probably put it in a huge box and at the bottom of the pile. But then again, maybe not. I know Della was probably angry that the watch hadn't surfaced yet.

Della opened the last two boxes. Just another cashmere sweater and scarf and a pair of Gucci sneakers.

But no gold Rolex wristwatch.

Della couldn't believe it. She had hinted and hinted, and after all that, she didn't get it.

I overheard Della muttering to Weezy, "All the other presents are worthless. I am totally depressed. Screw my new leaf."

Della asked me if she could leave. She said she wanted to visit some friends in Beverly Hills. What she really wanted was to get the hell out of the house and get wasted.

I called a taxi and walked her to the street. I was furious.

"You are an ungrateful daughter," I said. "Margarita and I tried our best to make this a happy birthday for you. We both took time out of our busy days *for almost a week* to pick out things you would like."

"Margarita has busy days?" said Della with a sneer. "Give me a break."

"So you didn't get your watch. So what? You got other great presents. Great presents. Your presents are expensive and beautiful. Other kids would be thrilled to receive presents like the ones you got. Margarita and I went to dozens of stores searching for gifts we thought you'd be thrilled to receive. We spent *hours* doing that. And more hours wrapping the damn things, and you pull this . . . this . . . *attitude*! You don't say thank you. You don't say anything. Not an ounce of gratitude. Just a miserable expression on your face and a miserable mood. Well, you can take your expression and mood and stick them in your ear."

"I *told* you about that watch ages ago," said Della, fairly spitting the words out of her mouth. "You and your miserable Margarita could have bought me the watch, then I would have *really* been happy. But obviously all you thought about was having fun with miserable Margarita."

The taxi arrived. Della opened the back door and slid into the seat, sulking up a storm, slamming the door behind her. Just before the taxi pulled away, I threw a box onto her lap through the open back window.

It was the gold Rolex wristwatch.

9

"There's someone who finally cares about little ol' me," Della told a friend. "Someone who honestly cares. His name is Billy. He wants me to give up drugs. He wants me to stop smoking. He wants me to try harder in school. Billy thinks I can be the doctor he couldn't be. Billy's the best influence on me I ever had. Because I like him so much, and admire him so much, I do what he tells me to do."

As far as I was concerned, there were three scary things about Billy. He was a high school dropout, a construction worker, and he drove a Harley-Davidson motorcycle.

Della described Billy as big for sixteen. She said he was six feet two and weighed close to two hundred and twenty pounds. He had been a football star for Beverly Hills High School before he dropped out. He wasn't fat. He was all muscle. A real *shtarker*. That's because during the summer Billy had been working for his father, who owned a construction company. Billy was basically a loner who didn't have many friends. He didn't care much about friends. What he cared about was his family obligations, Della, and his Harley.

Billy was a gentleman and a scholar. I wasn't aware of that until it was too late.

"I want to meet this boy you're so serious about," I told Della one evening. "But I've got to tell you, I'm not exactly jumping for joy that my only daughter is going with a construction worker."

Della told me one of the reasons she invited Billy to our house was because she thought Billy would be the kind of guy I'd like. She said, "I keep thinking Billy's a lot like you, Daddy, hardworking, a self-starter, stuff like that. I'm convinced you'll see the same things in Billy you saw in yourself when you were Billy's age."

When I arrived home the afternoon of "the meeting," I spiraled instantly into a black mood at the sight of the Harley-Davidson parked in our driveway. I always equated motorcycles with Hells Angels and guessed that Della would someday marry a Hells Angel, or someone with a motorcycle. I was sure of that.

Billy was Della's age, sixteen, and good-looking in a tough sort of way. As far as I was concerned, Billy was low class. He wore a black T-shirt and a pair of green camouflage pants tucked into his army boots. There was a pack of cigarettes rolled up in one of the T-shirt sleeves. *Why couldn't he keep his cigarettes in one of his pants pockets?* I wondered.

From the moment I saw Billy in our living room I disliked him. My hostility was apparent to both Billy and Della. As far as I was concerned, Billy (who hadn't opened his mouth yet) wasn't good enough for my daughter. Looking at him, I could tell he would lead my daughter further astray. I couldn't see any resemblance whatsoever between him and me.

Billy stood up when I came into the room. I noticed that. Unfortunately he had been sitting in *my* chair. I took another chair and sat down.

"Billy," said Della, "my father."

"Nice to meet you, sir," said Billy.

"Tell me about yourself, Billy," I snapped, my voice filled with attitude. I could hear it myself.

"I *told* you all about Billy," said Della.

"I'm a construction worker."

"And what does your father do?"

"I told you that too, Daddy." Della heaved a long, loud sigh. I could tell she wasn't pleased with me. I wasn't concerned. Later that day Della would call me a pompous ass.

"My father was a construction worker," answered Billy. "He doesn't work anymore. He recently suffered a stroke."

"I *told* you all that too, Daddy," said Della, exasperated.

"Sorry to hear about your father," I muttered.

Billy didn't appear to believe I was sorry to hear about his father. He didn't say thank you.

"Dropped out of school, did you?" I asked. The question came out sounding like an accusation.

"Yes I did. I *had* to drop out of school. Even though my mother was working, there still wasn't enough money to cover my family's daily expenses, you know, my father's medical bills, stuff like that. We needed to find more work and I needed to pitch in and help out in any way that I could." Billy shrugged it off as one of life's twists and turns. "Obviously I want more out of life than working in the construction business, but that's the best I can do right now. I don't regret things, Mr. Barris. My main responsibility is to my family.

"Also I'm a Methodist. I hope you don't mind a Methodist dating your daughter. I go to church every Sunday. I've been trying to get Della to come to church with me." Billy chuckled to himself. "I don't drink other than an occasional beer with my buddies on weekends. I don't take drugs for the same reason I don't drink. I always want to be in control of the situation. I'm very much against drugs of any kind. I even complain about Della's smoking. I know Della wonders why she's drawn to a guy like me, but she is. I think."

"Most definitely," said Della, almost shyly.

I hadn't the faintest idea what Billy saw in Della and vice versa. The two apparently saw something. Actually, I suppose, they were in love.

"Seems Della is heading in that direction too," I said. "Dropping out of school, I mean. Do you think you're influencing her?"

"I've told Della she should stay in school, get good marks, and go to college," answered Billy. "As for me, I didn't have a choice. I had to drop out of school to run the family business. My family needed me. If I had a choice I would have definitely stayed in school. I've always wanted to be a doctor. I told Della that."

"And I told *you* that, Daddy."

Billy made a lot of sense. He came across much better than I had thought he would. But how was I going to let Della go out with a *construction worker*? Out of the question. My daughter could do much better than a construction worker. Della had told me what a good influence Billy was, how he had made her try to be a better person. Della was such a flake, I couldn't believe she was doing something sensible now. I knew what kind of boy he was. He was a construction worker and a Hells Angel. He was just saying what I wanted to hear. All the good stuff. The truth was, he probably got drunk every Friday night with his buddies, then went home and threw up. I refused to believe Della's raves.

Billy said, "May I ask *you* a question, sir?"

"Why ... uh ... yes. Go ahead," I said, confused by the new turn of events.

"Why did you ask me here?" Billy asked furiously. "You obviously don't like me. And you know exactly *why* you don't like me? You don't like me because I'm a construction worker. You don't like me because I own a motorcycle. You don't like me because I dropped out of school, even though I had to. And no matter what I tell you to make you like me, you won't. Della told you I was a construction worker, and had a motorcycle, and that my father was sick and that's why I had to drop out of school. You knew all those things before I stepped my foot in your living room. So my question is, why did you invite me to come to your house in the first place?"

Before I could answer, Billy walked right past me and out of our house.

I was startled.

Della was devastated.

She said, "I brought Billy home to meet you because I figured you would like him. But you didn't. You know why? I'll tell you why. Because you're not the same man you once were. You used to be great. Now you're a pompous ass."

"Della, I—"

"You ignored Billy's good manners, the way he stood up when you entered the room, the way he said 'sir' to you. Good manners couldn't beat a T-shirt with a pack of cigarettes rolled up in one of his sleeves, could it, Daddy? True, maybe it would have been better if Billy wore a coat and tie when he came to meet you, as a show of respect. But who knows, Billy may not even own a coat and tie. Besides, he wasn't coming to dinner, or asking for my hand in marriage. He was just coming by to say hello. At *your* request."

Then Della left the house.

At two thirty that morning, I was awoken from a sound sleep by a telephone call from a neighbor saying Della was drunk and being loud on their front lawn. I went to the neighbor's lawn to bring Della home.

Billy never called Della again. It wasn't long after Della was sure Billy was gone forever that she became mad at everyone. Della took her anger out on all of us. Me, Weezy, Judy, on some of the few friends she had at school, and on her mother. My arrogant attitude toward Billy, being against him from the start because of how he dressed, his tattoos, and what he did for a living, had soured Della on me, possibly for good and always. If I could let her down like that, where was the hope? Della was convinced that this boy was the best thing that had ever happened to her, maybe the best thing that ever would, but because I couldn't see it, Della had lost him. I'm sure her mother would not have done something as distasteful as call Billy in for a snotty "chat."

Years later, on a bench in Beverly Glen Park, Della said to me, "Remember Billy? He was the boy who came to the house on St. Ives Drive, and wore camouflage—"

"Yes, I remember."

"I used to put myself to sleep at night dreaming that Billy and I were married. I dreamed we had a wonderful life together. We laughed a lot and hugged and kissed all the time. I dreamed the two of us had four boys: Matthew, Mark, Luke, and John. Billy and I knew we'd have boys and those are the names we decided on. Thinking about our family was a wonderful way to put myself to sleep. Now years later, when I'm all grown up, I still dream about Billy and the life we *almost* led. If it hadn't been for you, Daddy, if you hadn't stuck your nose into it, that would have been my life. I wouldn't have been sick. I would have—"

"I know," I said. "That was a big mistake on my part."

"Not a big mistake, Daddy. A tragic mistake."

From the moment Billy left our house in a fury, Della couldn't seem to bear the sight of me. Or my house, or Judy Ducharme. She was against everybody and everything. You could cut the tension with a knife until Della did something about it.

She took as much money as she could find in the house, money from my wallet and money from our housekeeper's wallet, put a few of her belongings in a knapsack, and ran away from home.

10

I knew Della had run away from home. I didn't know what to do about it all day. I was stunned, frozen, paralyzed, petrified. I couldn't function. I sat for the entire first evening in my armchair, staring at the walls. I did absolutely nothing. I was just worried. I was constantly worried. I wandered around my house muttering "another goddamn nightmare" over and over to myself. I thought, *What will people say? What will Della's mother say? What will the police say about my not reporting my daughter missing for almost twenty-four hours? I'll tell them this isn't the first time she's stayed out late. I'll just say I thought she was staying out late again, and I fell asleep. Makes sense.*

The second day, I thawed out. I went to the office and began making the telephone calls I should have made the night before. I called the police, all the hospitals. I had my secretary Loretta help me do it. There was no one around to help or advise me. I was alone. The closest people I could ask for help, my mother and sister, were three thousand miles away in Philadelphia. I was behaving like a wimp. I wanted my mother.

Della spent most of her first afternoon bumming around East L.A. looking for a place to stay the night. She didn't find anything cheap enough for her budget. She didn't want to blow all the money she stole from home in a couple of days. She spent the first night on the street. She slept in an alley. She was lucky, it was a warm night. Nights could get chilly in L.A., but not that night. That night Della slept well.

The next day was just like the first. Della wandered the streets, looking through trash cans for a hunk of cardboard to make a sign saying I HAVE NO MONEY AND I'M HUNGRY. She sat with the sign for a couple of hours leaning against a downtown Los Angeles building. She didn't collect much money.

That night Della went back and slept in the same alley she slept in the night before. Once again it was warm, but that's where the similarities ended. She might have slept the entire night if she had the chance, but that night Della didn't sleep.

Sometime in the early hours of the morning, she was kicked awake by a boot in her ribs. From where she lay, gasping for breath, she counted four legs. There were two guys standing near her. Both were white and drunk. One was skinny, the other was bigger, fatter, flabbier. The two of them had tattoos and shaved heads. The skinny one had two front teeth missing. The fat one had a cleft palate.

The fat one pulled Della to her feet by the collar of her jacket. He flipped her around so that Della's back was to him and he locked his arm around her neck. Della told me she could smell his body odor and whiskey breath. She and the fat one watched while the skinny one went through her duffel bag. The skinny one with the missing teeth looked meaner than the fat one. Della watched the skinny one find her money, watched him flip a self-satisfied smile to the fat one holding her in his armlock.

The fat one's armlock grew tighter and tighter. Della thought he was going to choke her to death. She was getting dizzy and felt faint. She thought she saw the other one put her money in his pocket. She tried to pull the arm away from her neck with both hands so she could yell at the skinny one, but she couldn't. The fat one was too strong. Della was sure she was going to die. She was so scared she peed her pants. When she did, the fat one let her go.

Della told me later, "If I knew that, I would have peed earlier."

The fat one knew what Della had done. He could feel her wet urine against his leg, see the stain on his jeans. The fat one told the skinny one, "The bitch just pissed herself."

The skinny one laughed and said something Della would never forget. He said, "Just like hangin' a cat."

Della screamed at the skinny one holding her wallet, "Give me back my money, you toothless jerk."

The skinny one stood, walked over to Della, and punched her in the nose.

Della said she literally saw stars and sat right down on her backside. The punch didn't hurt at first and then it hurt a lot. Della's nose was broken. She kept swallowing blood. While she cried and choked on her blood, the one who punched her angrily pulled Della's gold Rolex watch off her wrist. He pulled it off without opening the clasp. The bracelet, though loose, made long bloody slashes on Della's wrist. Then the two started to walk away.

Della said she leaned back against the warehouse wall and sobbed. She said she looked up at the black sky and asked God, "What's to become of me?"

He didn't answer.

The morning of her mugging Della returned home. When she realized quite clearly that Billy was gone forever, Della's anger was helped by the fact that every time she inhaled she felt a searing pain in her side. The pain was caused by the skinny hoodlum's initial kick to her side and the two broken ribs that had resulted.

Because I was the cause of Billy's disappearance, Della thought I was the biggest pain walking. I wasn't the only one, or thing, she resented. She disliked her room, her clothes, our Hollywood house, and the few friends she had. Della always reminded me about my beach house in Malibu. "That was my favorite house in the whole world," she said over and over again, rubbing it in, knowing how sorry I was that I had sold that house.

Della returned to Beverly Hills High after her brief but awful two days away from home. She promised me she would be good at school and not do anything stupid. She also promised to see a psychiatrist. She made those promises to me so I wouldn't punish her for running away from home. I thought her broken nose was punishment enough. I was heartsick about her nose. I was worried that it would never look the same again. I was right. It never would.

If school had been miserable for Della before, it was worse now. Della always wanted to be the talk of Beverly Hills High School. Well, she was when she returned, and it wasn't good. It was all bad. Word had gotten around about the mugging. Not hers, but the one she had given her classmate. Everyone was talking about how Della and her gang had punched and slapped the girl around so much she'd had to go to the hospital.

Della had not only become known as a druggie but also as a habitual troublemaker, someone who *attracted* trouble. Bad kids gave Della an even wider berth than the good kids. Even her old gang figured if they hung out with Della they would be watched more closely than ever, so they avoided her too.

Della longed to return to the Horace Mann School in New York. Suddenly that's all she talked about. That, and about how she didn't want any part of me or Los Angeles anymore. She begged me to allow her to go back to her mother and the life she lived in New York City. She said she hadn't realized how good she'd had it before, living with her mother in Switzerland and New York. She said she wished she was anywhere but in Los Angeles with me.

I reminded Della that she had told me over and over again how much she hated living in New York with her mother. Della said I was wrong. "Besides," she said, "I never wanted to live with you. Not really. I never asked you to take custody of me. You're a nonperson, Daddy. I never see you. You go to the office before I wake up and come home after I go to bed. You poke your head in my bedroom and if I'm up, you say something junky, like, 'How was school today, honey?' or 'Are you my favorite person in the whole world?' and that's it. At least my mother was around. Now Judy Ducharme takes care of me all the time. Judy's *not* my mother. *Or* my father."

Though I always spoke of Della affectionately with others, at that point I truly despaired of her. I found the responsibility of caring for my daughter loathsome. Also, Della's discussions about returning to New York and being with her mother were getting on my nerves. "Mom never laid down any laws," she said. "She wasn't even concerned about my grades. Not really." For a while that's all Della talked about: how much better she would be with her mother than with me.

Those were bleak days for both of us. I was lost. So was Della. I felt my future with her was hopeless. I'm sure she felt the same way about me.

11

The psychiatrist's office was in Brentwood, in one of those low-rise medical buildings. Della and I went together from home. We drove partway, parked, then walked. Our appointment was at eight a.m. to accommodate my need to get to my office early. As usual, Della was wearing an outlandish outfit that embarrassed me. I'm sure she was wearing the outfit to do just that. She had on a big khaki rain hat, a black T-shirt that had a dumb saying printed on the front, something I've forgotten but remember as being really stupid. She had on knee-high red socks and some old army shoes. Della seemed amused by it all. I wasn't. She carried a backpack over her shoulder.

While walking to the psychiatrist's office Della said, "Didn't we both adore each other at one time, Daddy? Didn't we laugh and have fun together? Wasn't I your best friend? How did our father-daughter thing get so screwed up? Am I really a walking nightmare?"

"Maybe we got off to a bad start when you overdosed as soon as you came to live with me? Or how about running a gang of high school thugs? Or shoplifting? Or your out-of-control use of drugs and alcohol? Or never listening to a thing I tell you? Or your playing one parent against the other, your lying, banging up my car, running away from home? Maybe, just maybe, those things have something to do with the way I relate to you these days?"

I remember thinking to myself, *I'll bet that wasn't the right thing to say at this moment in time.* I'm not sure, but I think Della was asking for forgiveness. Maybe it was the time to try to make amends. Maybe.

Then Della interrupted my thoughts with a startling question: "Would you be happier if I were dead?" she asked.

Jesus, what a question, I thought. "Let me ask you the same thing. Would you be happy if I were dead?"

"Answer me first," said Della. "I asked first."

"That's a really stupid question, if you ask me," I said. "No, I would be devastated if you died." For a split second I wondered if I was telling the truth. "And you?"

"Well," said Della, "sometimes I put myself to sleep at night dreaming you're dead. Heart attack or something. All of a sudden everybody pities me, which is a new thing for me. Also I inherit all your money and I buy myself all sorts of goodies. I drop out of school and buy a house somewhere else, maybe in Italy or Colorado, and live happily ever after. But I don't know if I would feel that way if you *really* died."

My God, what *had* happened to the two of us? I wasn't sure at all what to do anymore or how to handle Della. Had I been too hard on her? Was I being a good parent? A threatening one? Did it make any difference?

The doctor's office was one flight up, and down a long narrow hall with rows and rows of doors. Every door had a bronze doctors' name plaque on it. One of those offices was the one we were looking for. The name on the door read "Dr. Mortimer Rosenbloom." Friends told me Dr. Rosenbloom was the best child psychiatrist in Los Angeles.

The two of us walked into the doctor's waiting room and sat down. Della put the knapsack she was carrying on the floor between her legs. I sat down beside her.

"You look tired, Daddy."

"I didn't sleep well last night."

Della seemed to want to give me a hug. But just then a smiling man opened a door to the side of us and said, "Hi, Della. I'm Mort Rosenbloom." He seemed excessively cheery.

Della muttered, "Hi." She was looking down at her shoes.

"Please come into my office," said Dr. Rosenbloom to Della.

"Said the spider to the fly," mumbled my daughter.

"What?" asked the doctor.

"Nothing," said Della.

I got up to go into the doctor's office with Della, but Dr. Rosenbloom said, "Just Della. We're going to be about an hour. Why don't you go downstairs to the coffee shop and get yourself a cup of coffee."

"I'll just wait here," I said.

Later the psychiatrist returned to the waiting room and told me what had happened in his office.

"Della walked in with her canvas backpack over her shoulder," said the doctor. "I told Della to make herself comfortable. I showed her to an armchair. She sat down and put her backpack between her legs.

"Della said, 'You look like a nice man.'

"I told her I was.

"Della said, 'So what? My father looks like a nice man too.'

"I made a note of Della's hostile reply. Della seemed impressed with all my degrees hanging on my walls.

"Your daughter said, 'I guess Daddy picked a winner.'

"Then Della pulled a Nikon camera out of her backpack and said, 'Mort, can I take a picture of you?' That kind of took me by surprise. Both being called Mort and being asked whether she could take a picture. I guess your daughter called me Mort because that's the way I introduced myself. I didn't say, 'I'm Dr. Rosenbloom.' I was a bit ill-at-ease, mostly at your daughter's request for a photograph, and said, 'Certainly.' Then Della said, 'Say cheese,' and I became totally discombobulated. I may have even rolled my eyes." Dr. Rosenbloom gave an embarrassed laugh at the thought of rolling his eyes in front of a patient.

The snapshot Della took of her psychiatrist (which I never saw) must have looked exactly like someone who was a psychiatrist. Dr. Rosenbloom had thick curly hair with a wide friar's circle of bare skin in the middle of his scalp, tortoiseshell spectacles, and a bushy black beard. He was wearing a checked woolen shirt, a weird-looking tie under his tweed sport coat, and the thick-soled black shoes that policemen usually wear. The sport coat had suede patches on the elbows.

"After taking the picture of me," said the good doctor, "Della put her camera in her backpack and put the backpack between her legs.

"I took a pipe from my pipe rack and began telling Della how my doctor made me stop smoking a pipe. I was going on about what the doctor said, when suddenly I . . . uh, I stopped talking and was truly shocked at what I saw. Della had reached into her backpack and pulled out a baby's bottle full of milk, complete with a rubber nipple. She began sucking on the bottle. She did that without ever taking her eyes off me.

"'That's clever,' I told Della, 'you're showing your disdain for me, right? Well, I must say I've never seen disdain expressed in such an original manner.' Della said nothing. Just continued sucking her bottle. 'So please tell me, Della,' I said, 'how did you come to such a remarkable and creative way to express your feelings about this visit?' Again she said nothing. Just continued to suck her bottle of milk.

"I said, 'Let's talk about something else. Tell me about your parents. How do you feel about them?' Della continued to say nothing. Just sucked on her baby bottle. Eventually I grew impatient and angry. I believe I actually said, 'I give up.' I've never said that before. That's when I led Della back to the waiting room, to you. When Della knew she was leaving my office, she put the bottle back in her backpack. I suppose she didn't want you to see it."

"You *did* look a bit horrified when you came back to the waiting room," I said.

"Yes . . . well . . . this much I know, Mr. Barris. You have a bipolar, drug-addicted tiger by the tail."

Not long after I took Della to the psychiatrist, she showed up unexpectedly at my office. Everyone there was glad to see her though somewhat disconcerted by her appearance. Once again, she was dressed like some sort of ragamuffin. My secretary Loretta gave her a big hug. She said later that Della looked troubled.

Della knocked on my door. I hollered, "Come in."

She opened my office door but stood in the doorway. She leaned against the frame and told me she wanted to drop out of school and leave home.

"But you're only sixteen," I said.

"I'm old enough to leave home if I want to and drop out of high school too," she said.

Little did I know that the snapshot God took—Della standing in my office doorway, me sitting at my desk—I would remember for the rest of my life.

Della looked so sad.

I know now what I should have done and said. I should have walked up to her, taken her into my arms, given her a big hug and a kiss on the top of her head, and said as forcefully as I could, "You will *not* leave home. You will stay with me and return to school. You will give up drugs, and you and I will stick together. I am *not* about to give up on you. Nor will I allow you to give up on me. So get that idea out of your head about leaving home and school, do you hear?" Something like that.

And that's exactly what Della wanted me to say.

Instead I said from my desk chair, tired and weary of the worry and aggravation, "Fine. If that's what you want, then go. I'll set up a trust fund for you to live on. Okay?"

"Okay . . . I guess," she said. Her voice sounded like a little squeak.

Weeks later, Della hitched a ride from her small apartment in Brentwood to Doheny Drive. That's the street that snaked its way up the Hollywood Hills to St. Ives Drive, where our little upside-down house was. It happened to be a steamy California day. Della walked the long, steep hill up Doheny to St. Ives Drive to our house to pick up some of her belongings. She rang the doorbell. She was hot, sweaty, tired, and disgusted.

Weezy answered her ring and threw her arms wide open, just like she always did. Della climbed into Weezy's arms and was rewarded with a big hug.

"I just need to get a few things out of my room," she said.

Weezy looked frightened.

"What's the matter, Weez?" Della asked.

"We put everything of yours in boxes and sent the boxes to storage."

"*All* my things, Weez?" Della said, shocked.

"I told your father you'd be angry," she said, "but his girlfriend insisted that—"

Della went immediately to her room. Everything was gone. Everything. Her nernies and doohickeys from her night table. Her collection of greeting cards from the top of her bureau, her stuffed animals from the foot of her bed, and all her snow globes from the fireplace mantel. Even her favorite comforter. Della's old bedroom was now a guest room.

Della told Weezy her room looked like something you'd see in a cheap motel. Weezy said Della stood at the door of her old bedroom, crying and moaning, for a long time. Weezy said, "Della was so hurt it was pathetic."

Della left the upside-down house on St. Ives Drive and never came back.

12

It was 1982. Della was nineteen years old. She telephoned me at my office and said, "Daddy, I want you to give me away."

"Give you to who?"

"Daddy, I'm getting married and I want you to give me away. Fathers give their daughters away. It's an expression."

"You're getting *married*?"

"Yes. Is that so unbelievable?"

"No. No. I'm just . . . you always . . ."

"Will you pay for my wedding, Daddy? Fathers are supposed to pay for their daughter's wedding. A simple yes or no will suffice."

"Who's the boy? What's he do?"

"His name is Tony. You obviously haven't met him and don't know him. I'm not sure you know *me*. He lives with his family in Brentwood. He wants to be an architect."

"An *anarchist*? The boy's an anarchist?" I asked.

"An *architect*!" she yelled. "Damn it, Daddy, you're getting deafer and deafer by the day. Tony's taking some night courses now and—"

"All of a sudden she's getting married," I said, more to myself than to Della.

Della started crying. "Maybe if I was still living with you," she said between sobs, "like I should be, you would know something about me. Maybe if I was living at home, or if we had seen each other a couple of times during the last four years, you would understand who I am and what's happening in my life. You might even be familiar with the man I'm going to marry. None of this would come as such a tremendous shock to you. Anyway, the guy I'm marrying, his father refuses to pay for the wedding. Besides, it's the *bride's* father who pays. Just answer me. Will you give me away and pay for—"

"Yes. Yes. I'll give you away and pay for your wedding. You make the arrangements and send me the bills."

Tony was Della's first serious boyfriend since Billy. The only difference was, Della loved Billy. She didn't love Tony. At all. Nor did Tony's family love Della. Della called him Tiresome Tony. He came from a long line of German Jews. German Jews, according to Della, are bred to be uptight, boring creeps.

When Tony brought Della home to meet his parents for the first time, they thought their son had gone stark raving mad. They couldn't understand what their son saw in Della Barris, dressed as she was in her usual lunatic style and made up like some kind of prehistoric creature. And Tony hadn't even mentioned that they were thinking about getting married.

Della was convinced Tony was going with her and eventually would marry her because he had heard a rumor she had run into big money. In Della's opinion, that was the only reason Tiresome wanted to be with her. The reason didn't bother Della. Mainly because, as Della was quick to tell her friends, Tiresome was sex crazed and incredible in bed. "He's not the least bit tiresome there," she was happy to say.

Della was surprised she said yes when Tony suggested they go steady. But then she wanted to go steady with *someone*. Scrounging dates every weekend was not her cup of tea. And maybe someday she'd marry Tiresome, and then she could start her own family and have her own children. Little people to love the way she loved her little doggies. If Tony eventually proposed, Della would accept. Why not? When Tiresome got on Della's nerves, which he most certainly would, and she couldn't stand being around him anymore, which was bound to happen, she would divorce Tiresome and take him to the cleaners. Della never considered that the reverse might happen.

Della told friends that Tony wasn't good-looking and wasn't ugly. He was like, eh? Mr. Everyblahman. He could be an ax murderer or a clerk in a bookstore. He looked like every face in every crowd. He tried growing a mustache to give his face a distinguished look, but he still looked like Mr. Everyblahman. According to Della, Tony's 'stache resembled a used toothbrush with black bristles instead of white. Della wondered why he took the trouble to grow such a miserable-looking thing and why—after seeing it—he didn't just shave it off. Mr. Everyblahman, that's why.

They went to Tony's parents' house for dinner. It was the one night Tony's parents grudgingly allowed their son to bring Della to their dining table. Just that once and then no more. Tony was going to break the news that evening that he and Della were maybe going to go steady, and maybe eventually get married. Della told her friends Tony's parents hated her and detested the idea of her entering their house. Della said she pranced into their living room as if she were a member of the family, allowing them to see her for only the second time in their miserable lives.

"His parents appeared to be on the verge of matching strokes," explained Della to her friends, "which was really weird. I thought I looked cool as a cucumber. Orange hair, black eyeliner, fire-engine-red lipstick, the shortest miniskirt imaginable, and four-inch platforms. How bitchin' can one girl get? Anyway, we didn't tell Tony's parents we were thinking of getting married. Not that night. Tony chickened out."

Eighteen people came to Della's wedding. Tony and Della. Tony's mother and father, scowling the entire time. Tony's three older married sisters and their husbands. Some friends of Della's mother, me, and my date. The ceremony was held in the auditorium of a small synagogue in the neighborhood. At the party that followed the ceremony, Della's mother sat at a different table than I did. During the dinner festivities, I saw my ex-wife stick her tongue out at me. I thought that was very strange behavior on her part.

Tony's parents had Della's marriage annulled a month after the wedding.

"Well," Della said from her hospital bed, "having an abortion is one sure way of getting a family together. Abortions give dysfunctional families a chance to catch up."

"You've had an *abortion?*" said Della's mother.

"You had a *what?*" I boomed.

Della's mother and I had come to visit Della in the hospital. Neither one of us knew about the abortion until I heard my daughter say the word. Della's mother happened to be in Los Angeles visiting friends and called Della. Della had told her she was in the hospital but refused to tell her why. Della's mother telephoned me to say that Della was in Cedars-Sinai Medical Center.

"Why?" I asked.

"I don't know," said Della's mother.

My ex-wife asked me to meet her at the hospital. I said I would. I considered the trip to the hospital another installment in this long, continuous nightmare.

In the hospital, Della seemed to prefer seeing her mother. I don't think Della's mother liked me at all anymore. I don't think Della did either. Della's mother had aged. Her hair had gone gray. She looked old. For some reason or other I didn't like seeing that.

As if Della were reading my mind, she said, "You never seem to grow old, Daddy. I'm still waiting for the Dorian Gray thing to happen to you and your friend, Dick Clark. It's just a matter of time."

Isn't everything? I thought.

Della went on. "It's nice both my parents are taking a moment out of their selfish lives to enjoy each other, and me. I'm reminded of the old days, the happy days when we were a family and we all liked one another. Now my father doesn't like my mother, my mother doesn't like my father, and neither one of you likes me."

When I left Della's hospital room that afternoon, I wouldn't

see Della again for ten more years. And when I finally did see
Della, I wouldn't recognize her.

Della turned twenty-eight in 1990. To say she had changed was
putting it mildly. No more feeling sorry for herself. Any last in-
hibitions had disappeared. Now she was spending money, having a good time, living the good life. She had a sign made like
one that I'd had over my desk at the office. The sign said:

IF IT AIN'T FUN—DON'T DO IT

Della hung the sign over her bed. She told a friend of hers
she wasn't going to put up with anybody's crap anymore. "You
know what a guy I used to date told me? He said, 'You know,
Della, you're not an easy hang.' 'So, I'm difficult,' I said. 'So
what? I've had a difficult life.'"

The same friend told me, "Della went through a period of really feeling sorry for herself. She had about the lowest opinion
of herself anyone could have. She thought of herself as one of
those people nobody loved. She told herself she was worthless.
She moped around her one-room apartment in Beverly Hills
feeling sad and getting bored out of her mind. And if she wasn't
doing that, she was going to movies, or stuffing food into her
face, or screwing every guy who walked. It took months before
it dawned on Della what she was going to do." Della told her
friend, "My father pulled his tough-love gobbledygook, which
translated into giving me a lot of money to get rid of me. He
gave me a million dollars and told me not to come home until I
was 'drug free.' In short, get lost. If that's the way he wanted it,

that's the way it was going to be, with one major exception. I'm going to behave like all the other trust-fund jerkoffs I knew back at Beverly Hills High: spend it, flaunt it, enjoy myself."

According to her friend, "Della said she figured she could live well for a long time on a million bucks and have fun while she was living well. And that's what she decided to do. Della told me, 'To be suddenly rich does wonders for your soul. Before I was rich, I was sick of everything: my apartment, my face, my clothes, my life. What I was really sick of most was being me. I woke up every morning feeling sorry for myself, staring at my television set all day and night, drinking, snorting, and occasionally—only occasionally—mainlining, until I passed out.'"

Della's friend told me, "Della didn't think she was beautiful. She thought she was very Semitic looking. She had a busted Jewish nose and old-fashioned caps on her two front teeth. She said she decided to become a gorgeous Christian. She entered the world of plastic surgery. She said she could afford it, so why not? The first thing she did was get herself a nose job. She knew you loved her nose the way it was, even though it was busted, but Della said to hell with you and got it bobbed. When she was finished she said you could ski off it. She said she looked like a Barbie doll.

"Then," said her friend, "she had her teeth recapped, a chin tuck, a brow lift, collagen lips, her breasts enlarged, her eyes fixed, a tummy tuck, a bit of liposuction to get rid of the pounds she put on when she was depressed, her entire face tightened. The whole works.

"She had a professional hair stylist dye her hair platinum blond. Actually more white than platinum. When her face healed, she had a makeup specialist attack it. He put eyeliner around her eyes, gave her long fake eyelashes, and suggested she wear purple lipstick. As she walked out the door of his salon, she told me she heard one of the makeup guys say loud enough for everyone to hear, 'That girl looks bitchin'.' It was the first time, Della said, she had ever heard the word 'bitchin'' used when referring to her. She said, 'Maybe the guy's paid to say that every time a chick walks out of the salon.'

"Della told me," said the friend, "it took her close to an hour to put on her face. But in the end it was, as Della was fond of saying, 'Mar-vel-*loos*.' Della looked hot. She really did. She wasn't *beautiful*, but she had a look. A California look. She was so California, it was pathetic."

"What's a California look?" I asked Della's friend.

She answered, "I don't know, but Della definitely had it."

Her friends said Della dressed her own way, and in her own style. Wild colors. Wild clothes. She would go through an all-white period. Then an all-black period. Then a leather period. Then a multicolored period. Blouses, skirts, short-shorts, tank tops, and dresses in greens, yellows, purples, and reds. She constantly changed her hairstyle: this week long, the next week cut short. If she didn't like the cut, she wore a wig. She had her apartment painted all white. She bought all-white furniture. She even bought a white Mercedes convertible with personalized license plates that read HOTTIE.

Friends told me Della started going to discos by herself. She didn't need a date. She would enter the dance floor and everyone would yell, "Della's here!" That's when she'd strike her trademark pose: hands straight out from her sides, fingers splayed, legs apart, knees bent. Standing that way, she'd yell, *"Let's dish!"* I think it took a lot of nerve doing all the antics

Della performed. As I mentioned before, way down deep Della was like me, painfully shy. I know Della thought to herself, *Screw it. I can be shy when I'm dead. Now, while I'm living, I'm going to live.*

I was told Della learned to dance better than anybody walking the Sunset Strip. Boys *and* girls would be crawling all over themselves trying to dance with her. Della wasn't afraid to do anything: drugs, dancing, singing, taking a dare, or spending money.

As one friend said, "Della wasn't in school anymore. She wasn't an 'outsider' anymore. She was Della Barris—at last!"

Della was finally popular. Tons of people knew her name and who she was. She began to gain a following. That's because she was fun to be with. Her friends told me how you could always spot her whizzing around town in her white Mercedes Dellamobile with the convertible's roof always down, her dyed white platinum hair blowing straight out behind her, just like it had when I took her for rides on the freeways in my secondhand white Buick convertible.

I was told that during an amateur night at the Laugh Factory in Hollywood, Della, high on drugs, did an improvised stand-up comedy routine. The crowd loved her. Another night Della got drunk, climbed up on the stage at the Whisky A Go Go, and sang and danced. The band that was playing there let her stay on for more than half an hour.

According to friends, Della would be the life of every party she went to, and then just like that, she'd get bored and be gone. If she went to a boring movie, she would walk out. A boring rock concert, same thing. If the gang she was hanging with became boring, she split. Along with boredom, she hated disloyalty. If a friend did her dirty, he or she was dropped like a hot potato. "Gone with the wind," as Della liked to say.

Della dreaded anything having to do with death. Friends said she never went to wakes or funerals of family or friends. When she saw a hearse go by she would spit five times on the five fingers of her right hand, and say, "Poo, poo, poo, poo, poo."

Della adored Madonna. She knew all her songs by heart. She had Madonna's dance routines down pat. Della's friends swore she had better moves than Madonna. Della was passionate about her record collection. All of her albums were in pristine condition. Della would listen to them at night, pretending to be whoever was singing, using a hairbrush for a mike. Everyone's favorite expression regarding Della was "She's somethin' else."

Della loved Mr. Chow in Beverly Hills. She once got so wasted during a dinner there that she fell down the main stairway in front of a packed restaurant. The staircase led from the restrooms on the second floor to the main dining room. She jumped up after her slide down the stairs, struck her Della pose, and yelled to the stunned patrons, "Let's dish!" Then she laughed so hard she almost peed her pants. She told her friends she would have if she hadn't just gone to the ladies' room.

Her friends said Della wore bright red lipstick. She would kiss dogs on the mouth and laugh at the Kewpie-doll red imprint she left on their lips. She would fly to Europe whenever the whim hit her. She went to New York often. But as soon as she landed in the Big Apple, Della would start missing the California scene. And when she was finally bored with what she called "the ugly New Yorkers, particularly the ones who lived on the West Side," she would fly back to her sweet L.A.

Della had a cousin named Mary Wagman, whom she called Mary Wags. Mary lived in Manhattan. Della loved Mary Wags. They had great times together, Della and her crazy cuz. In Della's opinion, Mary Wags was the only New Yorker who could have passed for an Angeleno. When Della would fly back to L.A., Mary Wags would announce to one and all, "Jesus left the building."

Della often said that was a great title for a book. "If I ever write my life's story that's what I'll call the book," she told her cousin. *Jesus Left the Building.*

13

December 24, 1992.

Della was thirty years old. She called me up sobbing.

She said, between sobs, "It's Christmas Eve. It's also my birthday, remember, Daddy?"

"Of course I remember. What are you crying about?"

"I'm all alone. I'm by myself and nobody cares."

"I care."

"If you cared so much, why didn't you call me and wish me a happy birthday?"

"I ... ah ..."

"I'm the big three-o today, Daddy. Yippee! I'm twirling my index finger around in circles by my ear."

"Happy birthday, Dell."

"Yeah," she said, "I'm writing some maudlin crap in my book this morning. The book is called *Jesus Left the Building*. My handwriting sucks, Daddy. It seems to be getting worse.

They're playing Christmas carols on the radio on just about every station. They have been for weeks! The carols are driving me nuts. I'm so sick of Christmas carols, it's pathetic. 'Silent Night.' 'Have Yourself a Merry Merry Christmas.' 'Deck the Halls with Matzo Balls.' 'Hark the Harelip Angel Sings.'"

I laughed.

"Barbra Streisand's singing 'O Little Town of Bethlehem' now. If I hear 'Little Drummer Boy' one more time, Daddy, I think I'll puke. The only time California sucks is at Christmas. It's eighty degrees outside. What's the temperature in New York now, Daddy?"

"Twenty degrees. It's freezing."

"That's what winter's all about. Freezing. It's not supposed to be eighty degrees on Christmas Day. It's supposed to be frightful outside. That's how the song goes. It's supposed to be frightful. It's supposed to be gray and cold. I miss gray and cold. When it's sunny on Christmas in California, it's demoralizing. It's miserable. I'm miserable. Really miserable. Shouldn't fires be going in fireplaces today? It doesn't have to snow. It just has to be frightful. It has to be depressing and miserable. Christmas should be so depressing, people want to run out and commit suicide in the streets. Don't more people commit suicide during Christmas than any other time of year? Not in California. In California people die of boredom.

"I passed a store on Wilshire Boulevard today and the store had little cotton puffs pasted to their front window and a reindeer for window dressing. Guess what the cotton puffs were. Snow! Can you imagine, the white cotton puffs were supposed to be snow. Talk about demoralizing. The sweet gay-basher, Anita Bryant, is singing 'The First Noel.' Remember when you used to give me twelve presents on my birthday and twelve on Christmas? Those were the days. Now you don't give me anything. 'Little Drummer Boy' is playing again for the forty-millionth time. God I hate that song.

"Barry Anders and I were supposed to go skiing up at Big Bear for Christmas. I haven't been on skis since my downhill days at the *école*. I was going to show Barry a thing or two. He told me for weeks what a great skier he was. Barry didn't know I could ski like a bat out of hell, or used to. But then Barry called and made some excuse, something to do with having to spend Christmas with his family. Which of course I don't believe. Barry Anders is Jewish, for Christ sake. What Jew stays home with his family for Christmas? Good-bye Barry Anders. Good-bye Tony. Good-bye Billy. Is there anyone left for me to date? Is there anyone who will actually go out with me?

"This one I like. Dean Martin's singing 'I've Got My Love to Keep Me Warm.'

"Bye, Daddy."

14

I sold my business, got married again, and moved to France. That all took place in the eighties.

I also wrote a book in the eighties called *Confessions of a Dangerous Mind*. Della liked *Confessions* but she liked *You and Me, Babe*, my first book and a love story, better. Della liked *Babe* because the book was basically about her mother and me. *Confessions* really bothered her. She wondered if I was truly a CIA hit man and if I actually did assassinate enemies of the United States. In some ways Della thought being an assassin was pretty cool. In other ways it scared her.

"I don't see you carrying a gun," she said.

"I guess I'm not in the CIA then."

"But if you are, what would happen if you really became fed up with me?" she would ask on the phone from time to time. "Not that you aren't already, but what if you *really* became fed up with me?"

Della was eventually convinced that I did work for the CIA. I had gone to Europe enough times to chaperone *Dating Game* dates and visit her at the *école*. I was always running off an hour or two after I arrived to do something or other. I never said why I had to go so quickly or where I was going. And Della never asked. She wondered if assassinating all those enemies of the United States stressed me out and contributed to my becoming such a lousy father.

It was the nineties now. Della was still living in her all-white apartment in Brentwood. The only change in her life, and it happened to be a big one, was her trust fund was disappearing. She had been spending too much money too fast. As a consequence I had installed Solomon Abraham, my accountant, to dole out Della's money to her and try to stretch out Della's trust fund as long as he could.

Della described Solomon as "a smelly, bone-thin, balding accountant twerp."

Solomon Abraham was Solly to his friends, but not to Della. She called him Solly Cholly because he was always telling Della he was sorry but she couldn't buy this or that. Della didn't like Solly Cholly one bit. As far as Solly was concerned, the feeling was mutual. Della complained that Solly Cholly was always cutting off her credit cards. When he did that, Della was forced to go to work. She worked as a carhop at Dolores, the drive-in restaurant on the corner of Wilshire Boulevard and La Cienega. She also worked as a part-time librarian. But she couldn't stand any of those jobs. She quit each one after about a week on the job.

She tried being a comedian. Della remembered her impromptu amateur night performance at the Laugh Factory and how the audience loved her. So on the spur of the moment, with some drugs thrown in, she went to the Laugh Factory and got herself a spot on the bill just a week away.

During that week, Della rehearsed her act in the living room of her apartment. She put herself to sleep at night dreaming she would break out, become the new smash hit comic of the year. She would get standing ovations, overhear people saying, "You gotta catch Della Barris at the Laugh Factory. She's terrific! She's going to be the next Carol Burnett. You can bet on it." Della fantasized that word would get back to me about what a rising star my daughter was becoming. "There goes Della Barris's father," she would dream people were saying.

Della decided to use one name: Della. The hell with Barris.

I was told the club was packed for her first show. A friend said she was nervous as hell when she walked out to center stage and began, and that it showed. She started her routine by saying: "My father kicked me out of the house and told me not to come back until I was brilliant. 'Don't darken my doorway,' he said, 'until you're a nuclear physicist.' If that wasn't tough enough he added, 'A drug-free nuclear physicist.'" The audience laughed. Della appeared thrilled but couldn't keep it up. She became less and less funny as time went on.

"My father did that tough love thing with me," she said. "You know, gave me money and told me to go away and not bother him anymore. Then suddenly my father took sick. He was dying. I sat by his bedside and held his hand. 'Della,' he said. 'I have something to confess.' 'There's no need to confess, Daddy. Rest, just rest.' 'No, I want to die in peace. I must tell you. I've been a terrible father. I gave you money so that I could get rid of you.' 'I know, Daddy. Now rest and let the poison do its work.'"

Della expected everyone to roar with laughter, but no one did. Maybe because it was an old joke. It was very discouraging to hear a sprinkling of chuckles and hardly any applause after her last joke of the evening. Della was a mess when she walked off the stage.

"I was bad because I was nervous," she told one of the other comics.

"Don't worry," said the comic, lying. "The crowd was sitting on their hands tonight."

The next night was the same. Bad. And the next. On her last night she got high on some amphetamines before she went out on stage. She may have taken too much. Someone told me Della was a disaster. Another comic had to come and pull her off the stage in the middle of her act while the audience yelled terrible things at her.

She told a friend, "I wasn't disappointed that I had failed so miserably. I was mortified."

After that, Della worked as a "food processor" at McDonald's and Denny's. "Food processor" is a fancy title for putting together a customer's order. Then she became a salesgirl at Victoria's Secret and Theodore. Theodore was a hip store for men and women. All the salesgirls wore tight white T-shirts and tight white jeans with no underwear so there wouldn't be any bra straps or panty lines showing.

Eventually Della was fired from all those places. At Denny's and McDonald's, she was always eating. At Victoria's Secret and Theodore she was accused of having an "attitude problem" and stealing. Maybe drugs were the cause of her hunger at Denny's and McDonald's and her "attitude problems" at Victoria's Secret and Theodore. Even Solly Cholly quit being her accountant. He said, "Enough's enough."

And then, as if her world couldn't have become blacker, she met Strickland.

"Isn't that what usually happens?" Della told a friend. "During bad times you meet bad guys and during good times you meet good guys?"

Della was down on her luck when she met Strickland. There would come a time when Della wished she had never heard his name. Or that she'd had the good sense to turn him away when she first met him. Every snapshot she had of Strickland clearly showed a mean and nasty man, which is exactly what he was. Mean and nasty. Like one of those mean, brown pound dogs with black muzzles that bare their teeth when you come too close.

It was obvious to everyone that Strickland was a scumbag. Della knew that. Someone told me Della simply figured that at that time in her life she deserved him. I didn't agree. I always figured Della knew exactly what she was doing. I think Della was doing the monkey thing: see no evil, hear no evil, speak no evil. Why? Because Strickland was getting Della all the drugs she could pay for on a regular basis. That's a good enough reason if you're a junkie, which Della was. The bad part of the deal? She had to pay for her drugs. Strickland wasn't about to do Della any favors. And Della was running out of money. Eventually Della got herself good and hooked on coke, which was bound to happen, mostly due to freebasing.

As someone told her, a bit too late, "When you start on crack, there's no going back."

"Remember," she told a friend later, "cocaine wasn't new to me. I tried it when I was fourteen and went to the hospital after overdosing at a kid's party in Beverly Hills. The point is, when a kid like I was starts on drugs, you've got to nip it in the bud, quickly."

Della was full of it. I tried to nip it in the bud, but she refused to go anywhere. She would run from rehabs and detox centers and from doctor's offices. Della was of a different mind back then. I should have sent her to a good hospital and had her cleaned out under penalty of death.

Shoulda, woulda, coulda.

Times were rough for Della. For one thing, she had spent most of her money becoming the "New Della." Now there was very little money left. Some, but not a lot. And Della was all alone in California. Her mother was living in London and I was living in France. Even Judy Ducharme was busy with a new boyfriend.

Della was feeling sorry for herself, and she had a right to. It was an awful time for Strickland to show up in her life. Della's troubles were mounting so fast, she could barely cope. Turned out Strickland was thinking Della had money and eventually would be able to support them both. He was terribly wrong, and when he realized it, he took it out on my daughter, yelling at her constantly, berating her, mouthing off all the time. Until the day she died, Della had no idea why she allowed herself to put up with the likes of Strickland. I think her love for the low-life Strickland was all part of the demolition derby that was Della's life. She said she didn't have a clue why she was so concerned about him. I did. Strickland was providing Della with drugs.

It wasn't long after Della met Strickland that she started going to pawnshops and secondhand stores with her jewelry, watches, and clothes. Della scrounged as much money as she could get from Solly Cholly before he resigned. Della even hocked her beloved Nikon camera, a present from her mother that she used constantly. She needed as much money as she could get to pay for her habit.

During the time Della was getting herself into big-time financial and health troubles, I was playing out my Walter Mitty fantasy in the south of France. I was living a boyhood dream pretending to be Hemingway and Fitzgerald, writing the Great American Novel in Saint-Tropez. Della thought I was nuts to sell my company and move to Europe. She didn't know it had always been my dream to write in the little fishing village of Saint-Tropez. My dear friend Larry Collins wrote there, and I had always looked upon his life with longing. I had promised myself I would do the same thing someday.

I saw the opportunity, and I took it.

Della told friends the new girl I was about to marry was a big sleaze. Della said she saw her walking in Beverly Hills with her mother and father. The girl didn't know Della but Della knew who she was. Mother and daughter looked like tough cookies. Della said the father was a slug. He appeared to be one of those henpecked husbands who looked as though he'd been run over by a Mack truck. The man's wife was obviously the truck. She was tougher looking than her daughter. She reminded Della of pictures she had once seen of the gangster Ma Barker. Della told me years later, in her mental snapshot of my about-to-be new mother-in-law, instead of a rolling pin in her arms, she would be cradling a Thompson submachine gun. Della said if she could make a bet, she'd wager hard cash that my future mother-in-law was going to cause me a ton of aggravation. To say nothing of her daughter.

Della was right, on both counts.

The girl Della saw on the street was the girl I married. I could see the woman was a grade-A lowlife *afterward*, but not before. Stupid me. I moved to France with my new wife. I bought a big home (my wife liked the house) in Saint-Tropez, overlooking the Mediterranean, and suddenly acquired the reputation for throwing lavish parties. Anybody at all who might know me would understand how much I hated parties. It was my new wife who loved parties. She was constantly seen in Paris, London, and Rome visiting the couturiers there. Della told friends she'd bet good drug money that the second Mrs. B. had a few boyfriends stashed in little apartments here and there in all of the cities she visited, ostensibly to see the new fashions. Della figured my new wife looked the type. Of course that was only her opinion.

And then one day I came home to find that my wife had taken off with one of our houseguests, Jimmy Nash, a very rich ne'er-do-well. My wife was heard saying at a beauty parlor, "My new boyfriend has more money than Chuck."

15

It was 1995. After the Nash catastrophe, I moved back to New York, in part to make up with my daughter.

"Neither one of us is getting any younger," I told Della on the telephone. I was in New York. Della was in Los Angeles. "It's time we made up and put our anger behind us. I want to see you. This 'estranged' nonsense has got to end. Late as it seems, I want us to have a real father and daughter relationship again, before I'm gone. You know what they say about life being short and all that stuff."

Della started to cry.

"Please stop crying," I said. "I hate when you cry."

Della seemed to stop crying.

I told Della I was coming to Los Angeles the following weekend. "That's when we will get together. I promise. I just want to hold you."

Della started crying again. I held the telephone away from

my ear. Then she stopped crying and told me, while blowing her nose, how excited she was that I was coming to see her. She said she was so excited she couldn't stand it. She made me promise to see her little apartment. I promised. She said she could hardly wait until we saw each other.

Della had moved out of the all-white place she lived in during her halcyon years. Now she was renting a much less expensive little efficiency: one room and a kitchenette on Dorothy Street. She told me she loved her new apartment more than her expensive "white palace." She said the new apartment was smaller, much cozier, and cute as a bug's ear.

As soon as Della finished talking to me, she called Judy Ducharme and told her about our telephone conversation and that I was coming out to California especially to see her and her apartment. She told Judy, "I can hardly believe it, but he's coming. I'm going to have to hang up now. I've got to spiffy this place up big time. My daddy's coming. My daddy and I are not going to be estranged anymore."

Judy asked what "estranged" meant.

Della said she didn't know but had a feeling it wasn't bad. She added, "Daddy and I aren't going to be apart ever again, other than living on different coasts."

Della's apartment was where she kept all the precious things she still had left: her record collection, some of her beautiful dolls, her guitar. Della thought again of our phone conversation and smiled. When Della finished cleaning, she sang some songs while strumming her guitar.

Della told Judy a few days later that she was thinking of using my visit as an incentive to get her life back in order. She would get rid of Strickland and try as hard as she could to stop taking drugs. She'd get a decent job, start living a decent life, start taking care of herself.

Della explained to Judy how she went through all her closets, took out of hiding various pictures and mementos of the two of us, mementos she had hidden away because the sight of them was too painful for her. She dragged out postcards and pennants she had saved, along with assorted baseball caps and a Philadelphia Flyers jersey that Bobby Clarke wore in combat, complete with bloodstains. She told me she never stopped rooting for the Flyers, the Eagles, or the Phillies, because her daddy was born and raised in Philadelphia.

I remember when I gave the Bobby Clarke jersey to Della. She was ten. That same year I took her to a hockey game between the Boston Bruins and the Philadelphia Flyers in Boston. Della proudly wore the jersey. In between the second and third periods Della went to get a hot dog. While in the crowds at the hot dog counter she was roughed up by some teenage boys who disliked the Flyers shirt. I went out looking for her and saw her being pushed and shoved by the young boys. I couldn't get over that. A ten-year-old *girl*! And I thought Philadelphia fans were obnoxious. Lovable in a bent sort of way, but obnoxious.

Della told Judy she found a large pin, with two ribbons, one red and one blue, hanging down from the big red-and-blue button that said PENN on it. I bought Della that button pin at the Yale Bowl when the two of us went to see Yale play Pennsylvania. My father, Della's grandfather, went to Penn.

Judy told me Della said she even had the Serendipity menu from the afternoon I told her I had gained custody of her. The menu was covered with chocolate stains. Della placed the menu where I surely would see it. She said there were several other pictures of the two of us. One showed us jumping up and down on my bed in a San Diego motel when we went to the San Diego Zoo. Another was a picture of the two of us standing in front of the Dorchester in London the night after I had my nervous breakdown. There were other photographs and mementos. Della told Judy a corner of her living room might have passed as a shrine to me.

Della bathed her three doggies Faith, Hope, and Charity. After their baths, Judy said, Della danced around her living room holding old Charity. The two danced to Etta James singing "At Last." When Della finished cleaning her apartment, the place really looked extra cozy. Everything was ready for my arrival.

Judy told me Della counted the days left before I was scheduled to come. Seven . . . four . . . two . . . *the day!*

I never came.

I telephoned Della from the airport on my way back to New York. I made excuses for why I couldn't come to her apartment as planned: a meeting that ran way over schedule, and then a plane I had to catch back to New York for an important meeting the next day.

All of it was a big lie.

I simply chickened out. I wanted to get back to New York. I expected some sort of scene between Della and me and didn't want any part of it. I never seemed to understand the devastation I would cause my daughter by being so inconsiderate. *Why*, I wonder, *did I do such things? Why did I cause so much sadness over simple promises, promises I could have kept with hardly any trouble at all?* I heard that Della was bitterly disappointed I didn't come; she stayed high for a week. She told a friend she was tempted to destroy the shrine she made to me, but didn't.

I telephoned Della a few days later and said I would be coming out the following Friday. I told her I would come by and pick her up at her apartment. I asked her to be waiting outside; that way we'd have more time to talk. Della started to say something about coming up and seeing her apartment, but I brushed the suggestion away. The odd thing is, I never would see my daughter's apartment, or the shrine she made to me, or her little dogs. Not as long as Della was alive.

Or even afterward.

"I want to see you and talk to you," I said, "and . . . and make amends. I only have about an hour, but that should be enough time to catch up."

"Okay, Daddy," she said. "An hour's better than nothing."

Imagine. I hadn't seen my daughter in almost five years and I told her I was allowing her an hour of my time. What an idiot I was. How thoughtless can you get? Besides, Della knew that when Friday rolled around, there wasn't any guarantee I would even show up.

It was late in the day, but sunny and warm, when I finally arrived at Della's apartment. I wondered if Della would be happy to see me. I beeped my horn the way I used to: *da, dada da, da da*. Della raced down the front steps of her apartment house to the pavement. She wore her black suede peaked cap. The cap would be one of the few things Judy found for me when she went to Della's apartment after she died. I've kept that hat. She wore a Gap windbreaker over a decent-looking dress. I got out of my rented BMW, stretched out my arms, and Della ran to me. I hugged and hugged her.

My eyes welled up. I prayed they would stay that way, just welled up. No tears.

I hadn't seen Della since she had all that plastic surgery done to her face. My beloved nose was gone. So were a lot of other things I thought were beautiful on my baby girl. She looked completely different. I didn't like the new look at all. Her hair wasn't her natural strawberry blond color. It was orange. Her chin was gone, or replaced, or something. She appeared gaunt and pale. She had become alarmingly thin.

"You look so thin, Della."

"My appetite's not great, Daddy. That's all. I love you."

"Have you seen a doctor?"

"Yes. I'll tell you all about it later."

"Tell me about it now."

"No. Please. Let's go to the park. Please."

"Della," I said, dropping my arms, "you . . . you . . . look . . . so *different*."

"It's been five years, Daddy." And then Della began to cry. She ignored the panicked look on my face. Her face was buried into my shoulder. All I heard was a muffled, "Why, Daddy? Why?" *Why what?* I wondered. I didn't know how to answer Della's question. I wasn't even sure what the question was.

I hugged Della as hard as I could. Eventually I held her out at arm's length and said, "You look great, Della. Just great."

Della took a dirty Kleenex from her pocket and offered it to me. I wiped my eyes and blew my nose. And then I couldn't help myself. I said, "My beautiful nose. What did you do to my beautiful nose? And your chin. What happened to your chin?

It's gone! And your strawberry blond hair. Your *hair*, Della, what happened to your—"

"Get over it, Daddy. I did what I did. I dyed my hair a shitty color. I *hate* the color of my hair. Don't worry, it'll grow out blond again . . . I hope."

It never did.

"But it's like, it's like . . . *orange!* Are you okay?"

"Let's just go to the park."

Della got into my car.

We drove to Beverly Glen Park in Bel Air and found a bench. We sat down side by side. Della squiggled over as close as she could get to me. She knew I wasn't happy with her orange hair and all of her plastic surgery, that I was doing the best I could to ignore her entire physical change and move on. But she also knew I kept looking straight ahead and not at her.

"Daddy, you took me to this park to teach me how to walk, didn't you?"

I nodded. "This was the place."

"Isn't that fortuitous. Is 'fortuitous' a word?"

"Yes," I answered. "It means something that happens by chance . . . I think."

Then I said, turning to look at her, "Della, I've been a terrible father and for what it's worth, I want to apologize to you."

Della whirled around to face me. "Daddy, did you just say you were a terrible father? You did, didn't you?"

"Yes I did."

Della sat mouth agape. And then she said, "You're right, you were a terrible father. And now that we've covered that, let's move on."

"I know apologies are worthless at this stage of our lives,"

I said, my eyes starting to tear again, "but I just wanted you to know that . . . that . . ." I couldn't finish.

"I wasn't blessed with great parents, was I? But then I wasn't a great daughter. It doesn't matter anymore, does it? That's all ancient history. We're here now. That's all that counts."

I took a deep breath, took off my glasses, pulled my sport coat sleeve across my eyes, and sort of half whispered, "It *does* matter. In any case I'm glad I said what I said. That was my sole purpose of coming today. To tell you that, and apologize."

And then we *really* began to talk. Back and forth we went. I would ask Della questions, and she would answer them. Then she would ask me questions, and I would answer them. The two of us tried to play catch-up for what seemed like centuries, tried to get to know each other again. At least a little bit. We spoke way past the allotted hour. It was dark and we were still talking. That's when Della told me many of the stories I mention in this book, and more. For most of the time I was enthralled. There were other moments when I could have killed my daughter.

"Why did you leave France, Daddy? I was hoping you'd stay until I could come and see your house. I always wished you'd invite me, but you never did." She sighed. "So why did you leave?"

"I was homesick for New York," I said. "I was tired of being an expatriate. I wanted sports scores the next day, not two or three days later. About you coming to France, I *wanted* you to come very much. It was just that she—"

"Don't sweat it, Daddy," Della said.

"She was a real bitch, that one was," I said, more to myself than to her.

"You could have stood up to her, Daddy. Been a man. Stuff like that, no?"

"Yes, I guess I could have. I just hate to fight."

"Sometimes you have to fight. Do you know where Mom's living now? I heard she's living in London."

"I don't know where she's living."

"Listen, Daddy. I promised myself I would tell you the truth about everything. *Everything.* If, after hearing all my horror stories, you don't want to see me again, so be it. At this point, Daddy, I'm too far gone to change for you or anyone else."

Della took a deep breath and continued.

"I'm a drug addict, Daddy. I've tried to stop but can't. I thought when I ran out of money, I would stop, but I didn't. They say when you hit rock bottom you quit. They also say, 'The only way back is after you're dead.'"

"That's depressing," I said.

"Yeah, I guess so. Anyway, I've hocked just about everything I owned to get money for drugs. And some things I didn't own."

"Meaning . . ."

"Things I shoplifted from department stores."

"You're going to get arrested, Della, if you keep that up."

"Shoplifting? Yeah, it's bound to happen. Maybe I'll be able to kick my habit in jail. That's a bad joke, Daddy, isn't it? Anyway, to add to my miseries, I'm living with a real scumbag."

"Why don't you throw the scumbag out?"

"I can't. He gets me drugs." Della smiled. "Drugs possess you, Daddy. They become your entire life. You live for drugs. It's all you ever think about."

"Have you done everything possible to try to . . . to . . . stop?"

"I've tried, God knows I've tried, but I can't do it. From time to time I think I'll drag myself into some rehab program before it's too late, but I never do. One of these days I'm going to. I'm going to get the incentive and go to some drug rehab place, tell them to tie me down and get me clean. But not now."

"Why not now?"

"I don't know. Like I said, they say you have to hit rock bottom first and I guess I haven't hit rock bottom yet. I'll bet it looks like I have to you, but I haven't. I'll try to stop when I do."

"How will you know when you hit bottom?"

"They say you know. Would you change anything if you could live your life over again?"

"Yes. I'd change a lot of things. A lot."

"What would be the first thing you'd change?"

"I would change the way I handled you."

"In what way?"

"I would have been tougher. And more affectionate. And more understanding. I think after all my experience with a kid on drugs, toughness, affection, and understanding are what's needed most. Not the way I was, always angry . . . and gruff . . . and ill-tempered. I would have kept you in Westlake. I would never have put you in Beverly Hills High School. Maybe taken a leave of absence from the company and gone off with you somewhere together. Hell, I could have afforded it. Maybe taken you around the world. Get out of Beverly Hills. I don't know. I would have done something radical. But at the time, I was just building my new company. It was hard for me to leave."

"You would never have left your business, not then, not when you were becoming so successful. Personally what I think is, I think it was a bad time for you to take custody of me."

"Yes, you're probably right."

"I think you're loaded to the bursting point with regrets," said Della. "In fact, if you ever write your memoirs you should title the book *Regrets*."

"Sounds that way, doesn't it?"

We talked and talked until it grew dark and cold.

"Della, maybe we should go home. It's getting cold."

"Daddy, before we go I have something else to tell you."

"What, honey?"

"I'm HIV positive."

"You . . . you have . . . *AIDS*?" I stammered.

"No. I'm HIV positive. Being HIV positive means I *don't* have AIDS . . . yet. I'm just susceptible to catching AIDS. I may end up with it. I take drugs for HIV. The drugs are supposed to be getting better and better. I'm taking some of the new drugs now. It's expensive but what can I do?"

"I'll pay for your drugs," I said quickly, still in shock.

"You already do, Daddy. You've been paying all my medical bills all along. And my grocery bills, and my drugstore bills. When I get the bills I send them to Loretta."

"Just make sure the money goes to the drugs that fight AIDS, and not . . . and not the other stuff."

"I don't control the money you send me for doctors', dentists', and drugstore bills, Daddy. I don't pay the drugstore. I just send the bills to you."

"Are you HIV positive from the drugs you took, you know, from the needles?"

"No, it's not from that. I don't shoot up, Daddy, if that's what you're asking me. I don't do heroin. I don't mainline, you know, put a rubber band around my arm and use syringes. I do cocaine. I . . . well . . . I just sniff the cocaine up my nose."

Della had promised she would tell me the truth. Now she wasn't, as I'd find out later.

"When did you start? I mean, when did you *really* start taking drugs?" I asked.

"It started at the *école*, in Switzerland. At the *école* we all had marijuana in our rooms. It was at the *école* that I first tried hash too. That was really weird. I was scared when I tried hash. I had a strange reaction to it. I've never used it again. When I moved to New York the kids I knew there freebased cocaine, for which the street name now is crack. Crack is rough. You get hooked on that, like I did, and stay hooked. When I moved to Los Angeles, I was amazed to see all the stuff the kids used. They do everything out here. They even mix speed with heroin. They called it 'speedballing.' That could kill you. You fly up on the methedrine and down on the heroin and end up someplace you should never have been. Sometimes dead. Oh, in Beverly Hills the kids have all their parents' prescription drugs to play with too. The parents, the mothers mostly, have tons of uppers, downers, and tons of pain pills. The kids find them in their parents' medicine cabinets. All the mothers in Beverly Hills seem to be nervous wrecks. Oh, and I've used a lot of Ecstasy too. Anyway, I'm not HIV positive from drugs, Daddy, but from being promiscuous. I'm a nymphomaniac, Daddy. I'm sure of it."

It was a stunning afternoon. I was upset and very angry. Almost nauseous. Maybe it all had been too much for me to digest. Maybe Della should have told me everything over a few days. But then she didn't know if I'd be here in a few days.

I turned to Della and said bitterly, "I wish I never took you out of Westlake and never listened to your lies about the place being full of lesbians. You know what I wish? I wish you *were* a lesbian and lived with another lesbian. At least you might have been healthier, happier, and much smarter. You might have even gone to a great college."

"Wow," said Della, sounding angry, "you must have been keeping that one stored up in your head for years."

"Yes, well . . ."

"I have something to show you, Daddy, some pictures I took, now that I'm making a clean breast of things. I went to Las Vegas for a couple of days a while ago." She opened her carryall and pulled out a batch of Polaroid pictures and handed them to me.

"What are these?" I asked.

There were a dozen or so pictures of Della and different men. Della was sitting on most of the men's laps.

"Why were you in Las Vegas?" I asked.

"It's a long story, Daddy."

"I'm not sure I know what these pictures repre—"

"I took all of these men to my room in a Las Vegas hotel," she said.

"Why?" I asked.

"Like I said, it's a long story."

I really didn't want to know, but I couldn't help myself. I said, "Explain it to me." Suddenly I was furious.

"I charged these men, and it was fun. That's all I was there in Vegas for, to have fun."

"What did you use the money for, Della? Drugs? You bought drugs with the money you got from those men, didn't you?" I asked, my voice full of anger. "You didn't go to Las Vegas to have fun. You went to . . . to whore around so that you could get money to buy more drugs. You were running out of money so you went to Las Vegas to prostitute yourself to make money to buy more drugs, didn't you?"

"Yes. That's what I was going to do with the money, but—"

"But what?"

"Two cops arrested us. I was with another girl. The cops arrested us for solicitation. What they were *really* doing was shaking us down. That's what they were really doing."

God knows what Della was thinking about when she gave me those Polaroids to look at. Why? Why did she do that? To get back at me for turning my back on her for all those years? To get even with me for being away from her for so long? Was the HIV messing up her brain? Or maybe the drugs were? Or perhaps she was demonstrating what a life without love will make you do? I was sick to my stomach. I thought I might throw up. I got up from our bench and walked away. All I kept thinking was, Why? Why? Why? Why? Why was she doing this to me now? What purpose was she accomplishing? My daughter was telling me she was a whore. A drug-addicted whore. I wondered if Della found a defiant joy in her atrocious behavior.

"I'm sure I became HIV positive on that trip to Vegas, Daddy."

Della took back her Polaroids.

"Why did you show me those pictures, Della?"

"I don't know."

16

It took me weeks to get over what Della told me in Beverly Glen Park. After some time had passed, I remembered the reason I came back to the States: to spend time with Della. Something told me now was the time to be with my daughter, no matter what. Della and I would return to Beverly Glen and our bench as many times as we could and talk.

I started making regular trips to Los Angeles from New York to see her. And when I was in Los Angeles, I began taking her places and events I wouldn't normally have taken her. One night I took Della to an evening honoring a friend of mine, Stanley Donen. The affair was at the Academy Theater and the place was crawling with celebrities. I introduced Della to everyone I could.

"I'd like you to meet my daughter," I said.

Della was very nervous. She wasn't used to attending elegant functions like that one and being introduced to important people. Della handled the introductions clumsily. She looked and acted ill at ease, and I'm sure she felt ill at ease. She made others feel the same way, and I wasn't exactly sure what to do about it.

The Academy was having a retrospective of Mr. Donen's films. In one of the films Gene Kelly danced with the cartoon character Jerry, of *Tom and Jerry*. I knew Della *loved* cartoons, and that she was going to like the *Tom and Jerry* piece, and that the film would make her laugh. I was right. The film did make her laugh. Della tended to laugh constantly at funny movies, and somewhat uncontrollably. She talked out loud too, a throwback from watching a lot of TV at home alone. She seemed a bit retarded and couldn't seem to control herself, maybe, I thought to myself, due to her drugged brain.

When Della went to movies, she generally tried to avoid clumps of seated people. She always tried to sit somewhere by herself. Della understood that talking and laughing in a theater filled with people would be extremely annoying to others, especially to those sitting close to her. She was aware of all that but I think unable to do anything about it. In this performance, the Donen retrospective, we had assigned seats, and Della's carrying on, her incessant giggling and talking, was visibly annoying to the gentleman sitting on her left. He would constantly turn to Della and frown. The man's wife bent forward often to get a better look at Della and send her scowling facial messages.

Della knew she was being extremely annoying to the couples around her but could not do anything about it. We were with friends of mine that night, as their guests, and I was embarrassed for them because of Della's shrieking. But I was trapped. If I took Della out of the theater she would be mortified. If we stayed, I would continue to be humiliated for the entire show. I decided to stay. It was a horrible night for me.

Not long after that disastrous event, I took Della to a regular movie. This one wasn't animated. It was just a funny film. We tried to sit where there were only a few people near us. Della started doing the same thing she did at the Donen tribute. She talked out loud and laughed a lot. Della usually laughed at things that struck only *her* as funny. A large, gruff man seated next to her wasn't as polite as the gentleman at the Donen tribute. He turned and told Della to shut up.

Della turned and said to him, *"You* shut up."

The man bent around Della and said to me, "Get this loon-bird kid of yours the hell out of this theater."

My arm shot across Della like a rocket and grabbed the man by the collar of his jacket.

"What did you just call my daughter?"

The man said, "Easy, partner. Easy."

A little later the man and his wife moved away from us.

I stopped taking Della to movies.

17

Della needed money for drugs.

She had to force herself to leave her apartment so she could look for a job. She tried all sorts of places but struck out everywhere. She telephoned me to ask for help. I was able to get Della a part-time position in a dress shop on the corner of Rodeo and Little Santa Monica. The owner was a friend of mine. But the owner had to let Della go shortly after she started. Della forgot to turn off the coffeemaker one night and the store almost caught fire. The coffeemaker was one of Della's few responsibilities. She couldn't seem to remember things as well as she used to.

Della's friends, the few she had, stopped inviting her to their apartments and houses. Della would steal things from their homes to pawn so she could buy drugs. She'd steal little things she could take out of her friends' homes in her pockets. One of her friends continued to invite her over but always patted her down before she allowed Della to leave her house. She knew Della was an addict.

When Della wasn't doing drugs, she was sleeping. She seldom spent money on food, rarely went shopping at the market. She bought drugs instead. She felt sorry for her doggies. They were becoming skinnier and skinnier, just like Della. Della and her three doggies ate mostly breakfast cereal. Sometimes, without being asked, Judy Ducharme would go shopping for Della. I would pay Judy back for the money she spent on Della's groceries. Della thought the food Judy brought back was worthless. She argued with Judy, told her to stop. Della said, "You're spending good drug money on stupid food. Besides, I don't even have an appetite."

One morning in 1995, when Della was thirty-two, she was having a cup of coffee at a local Starbucks. She was sitting by herself at a small bar that ran along the front window and looked up from her *L.A. Times* calendar section just in time to watch a brand-new silver Mercedes convertible with its roof down slide effortlessly into a vacant parking place. The driver stepped out into the street and headed toward the Starbucks entrance. Della recognized the man immediately and quickly dropped her head deep into the *Times*. But not quickly enough.

"Della!" said the man, stepping into the coffee shop. "It is Della Barris, isn't it? I saw you in the window."

Della looked up into the smiling face of Billy.

Billy, the construction worker I didn't think was good enough for Della. After I gave Billy the snotty third degree in the living room of our Hollywood house, Della never saw him again. That had been sixteen years before, an event I can still remember vividly. I don't think, way down deep, Della ever forgave me for that, and rightly so.

"It is Della Barris, isn't it?"

"Of course it's Della. Who do you think it is?"

"It's just that . . . that . . . I almost didn't recognize you. You've done something to your . . . did you get your nose fixed? You changed something . . . never mind," he said, embarrassed. "May I sit down?"

"Sure. Sure. Please."

Billy pulled out a chair next to Della and slid onto it. "How have you been, Della?"

"Good. And you?"

"Good. Real good."

"Well, you certainly look it," Della said. "I was watching you park your Mercedes convertible."

"I had a Toyota for years," said Billy, embarrassed. "I just traded it in."

"A Mercedes is nothing to be ashamed of, Billy. Anyway, I hear you've built half the houses in the San Fernando Valley. If you wanted to drive a Rolls-Royce you could, couldn't you?"

"Yeah, I suppose so. We've done pretty well." Billy knocked wood. "As a matter of fact, my wife Shirley and I just came back from a month in Italy. We rented a villa on the Amalfi Drive. So tell me, Della, you feeling okay?"

"Yes, sure. Why?" Actually Della was feeling terrible and getting worse by the minute.

"You just look very thin, and tired," said Billy. "You taking care of yourself, Della? You sure you're okay?"

"I'm HIV positive, Billy. I've lost a lot of weight and I *always* feel tired."

"Oh Jesus. I'm sorry, Della."

"Hey, it's not your fault," she said, then doing her *Goodfellas* impression, sneering and flicking her hand, saying, "Fugeta-boutit." A long silence followed before Della said, "Tell me about yourself, Billy. What have you been up to? You look very chic in your suit and tie."

"Yeah . . . well . . . I have to wear this outfit today. We're having a company stockholders' meeting this afternoon. I'm trying to wake myself up with a jolt of Starbucks coffee. I was working late last night. My little company is a big public thing now. In twenty minutes I have to go and conduct the stockholders' meeting."

"Congratulations, Billy. I knew you would do well. So you're married, right?" Della asked, barely able to get the words out of her mouth.

"Yes ma'am. I've been happily married for almost fifteen years!"

"Fifteen years." Della felt her stomach drop to her shoes. She could feel herself shaking. "My God, Billy," she stammered, "you must have gotten married when you were—"

"Eighteen. Two years after you and I broke up. Been married fifteen years. Can you believe it? Time flies, doesn't it? Shirl's my age. We have a couple of great kids, too. Two boys and Shirl's pregnant again. It's going to be another boy."

Della was sick and getting sicker. If it wasn't for her damn father, that could have been her life and not Shirl's. Della and Billy had often talked about the names they would give their kids. They also knew it would have been boys. They even picked out boys' names: Matthew, Mark, Luke, and John.

Della thought she might throw up.

"Here, let me show you some pic—"

Della ran out of Starbucks.

Judy Ducharme told me that that night Della's world fell apart. Running into Billy was devastating to her. She drank a lot of vodka that evening and snorted some of the hidden stash of cocaine she kept under a floorboard in the closet. The bastard Strickland came by. When he knocked with his cute little rat-a-tat-tat, Della screamed, *"Go away, you fucker,"* and threw a chair at the door. Her three little doggies ran into the kitchen.

He went away.

Della picked up her nice chair and examined it. The chair was fine, but there was a gouge in the door.

She telephoned Judy Ducharme.

When Judy answered, Della started to cry. She begged Judy to come over. Della told Judy she needed her. Judy was there in ten minutes.

18

Della was falling apart at the seams. She told me she hated getting up in the morning. She said if she didn't have to go to the bathroom she would never leave her bed. Ever. She guessed she was nearing rock bottom. Had she hit it? She wondered if she was losing her desire to save herself. If she was, would she be able to get help in time?

She once said to me, "I feel my soul will never be clean again."

Della's paintings reflected her inner turmoil. She would get out of bed sometime in the morning, paint for hours in her tiny apartment, then—with her face, hands, bare feet, T-shirt, and shorts covered with acrylic paint—she would go back to bed, fully dressed and exhausted, and sleep for hours. When she awoke again, she would stagger out into the living room and look at what she had done. Sometimes she was amazed. Most of the time she wasn't.

The canvases were often small nightmares. The colors were morbid: dismal blacks and grays, and blackish blood reds, with streaks of brown and purple. Della's paintings were populated with ugly, scary people. The figures were ghastly. Some wore shrouds. Some appeared ghostlike. Their faces were small nightmares with fanged teeth and eyes dripping bloody tears. Yellow saliva foamed in some of her characters' mouths, and they had deep black holes for eyes. Forked tongues dangled from their lips. Some of her landscapes were mixtures of earthquakes and erupting volcanoes. Some were lava slides filled with charred bodies and human skulls. Other paintings depicted floods, with bloated bodies here and there. I never saw them. Judy Ducharme described Della's paintings to me.

Her work was appalling to look at, according to Judy. Even Della couldn't understand why anyone would want to buy one of her paintings. But the odd thing was, Della's paintings sold almost as fast as she could paint them. They seemed to fly away from the buildings they were leaning against. Passers-by grabbed her work and paid twenty, thirty, and sometimes fifty dollars for them as if they were really good. Della never understood her buyers' apparent love for such depressing art.

Of course the money Della received for her paintings would go directly to Strickland, who would buy the two of them drugs, less whatever Della could hide for little treats for her doggies and herself.

Then I met Mary. Della was becoming too weak and sick to paint anymore. The simple act of going outside was a chore for her. The only time she would muster up the strength to leave her apartment was when my new girlfriend Mary and I would come to Los Angeles, call Della, and ask if we could take her to a restaurant for lunch or dinner. On those occasions Della always found the strength to go. It seemed I had finally found a girlfriend Della liked. No, loved. Wonder of wonders.

Whenever we were all going to meet, Della would dress in her most outlandish outfits, wearing the clothes she had purchased at a local Goodwill charity store. The store seemed to specialize in long black beaded dresses with trailing trains, big black hats with bizarre peacock feathers and extremely wide brims, and long colorful silk scarves. Della loved that junk. She wore those garments well, but never around Strickland. He thought any money not spent on drugs was a waste and would scream and curse at Della for spending *her* money on "crap like that."

When Della arrived to meet us at the Peninsula, where we stayed, she would make a grand entrance in the hotel's lobby. Della behaved as if she were the duchess of Kent entering Buckingham Palace. She would come swishing down the long hallway, past the bar and the reception desk, hoping to shock everyone with her la-dee-da attire.

She probably did.

Eventually she would arrive at the room where high tea was being served and make her second super-duper grand entrance. Mary appeared captivated with Della's gaudy arrivals. I wasn't as captivated. I was a bit uncomfortable and showed it. Mary would turn to me and say, "She's having fun. Let her be."

Upon seeing us, Della would assume a wide stance, bend her knees, push her arms out to her sides, spread out her fingers, grin, and say, "Let's dish!" Others, having high tea, would look at Della as if she had just arrived from Mars. Knowing Della as well as we did, we knew she was trying her best to be cheerful, but it had become an effort for her.

Della said she could tell from our reactions that we were getting more and more worried about her. "The look on your face says it all," she would say. She was right. Getting used to her debilitated state was hard. "Don't worry," Della would always say, "I'm fine."

Della was far from fine.

The three of us would spread ourselves across two small sofas and a small armchair in the Peninsula tea room. Della generally didn't have an appetite, even for the little crustless tea sandwiches, which she once loved. Over tea Della would regale us with stories and jokes. It was hard work for her in her run-down condition, but she seemed to enjoy making us laugh. And we laughed, often and hard. Mary had a southern accent Della loved to imitate. Mary's accent wasn't very thick but it was thick enough to make a difference. Della used Mary's accent in as many stories as she could. She could mimic Mary perfectly.

When the three of us went to dinner, we would usually go to one of the better restaurants in Beverly Hills. Often, toward the end of the meal, Della would fall asleep at the table, a result of not taking any uppers before she left her apartment. Della couldn't afford uppers anymore. She'd nod off, her chin dropping slowly to her chest, her mouth open, saliva sliding down her chin. It wasn't a pretty picture. I would generally panic. Mary would be calm. Mary was always calm.

When dinner was over, we'd wake Della up. She would make me take most of what we didn't eat home for her, including the rolls and butter. Then the three of us would leave the restaurant. Della was often propped up between us, as though she were drunk. She wasn't drunk, she was sick. We'd walk Della to our car and drop her off at her apartment.

"Della, what are you using for cash these days?" I'd always ask.

Della would shrug her shoulders and I'd slip her a hundred dollars. Della would take the money, kiss me on my cheek, kiss Mary too, and walk to her apartment's entrance. She was usually okay walking to her apartment. The fresh night air seemed to revive her. Before she disappeared out of sight, she would turn and wave to us. Mary would always wave back, swinging her arm back and forth out the car window like an upside-down windshield wiper. The two would wave until my automobile turned the corner. Mary told Della once that it was a southern tradition to wave until the one leaving was out of sight.

When we were out of sight, I would turn to Mary and say, "Della's going to spend everything I gave her on drugs."

Mary would agree but then say something kind about Della.

Della told me when she got back to her apartment she would get a second wind, do some coke and drink a little vodka or gin, and imitate Mary. Della would talk in a southern accent, much thicker than Mary's, and tell her three doggies everything that had happened. She'd tell them where we ate, what the restaurant was like, if any celebrities were there and if so, who they were, and so on.

Della would say to her doggies, "Now y'all please make dog-gone sure to keep wavin' your paws when one of your friends walks away from y'all, and keep waving until they're out of sight, heah?" The little doggies would listen attentively.

And then at some point she would just pass out, often waking the next morning in strange places and in a strange position. She once woke up in her closet with one of her legs bent under her in a weird way. Her leg was numb for the entire day. She must have collapsed in the closet when she went to fetch something.

After Mary and I had returned to Manhattan, Della would phone us constantly. Mary loved getting her calls, when she could understand her. Often she couldn't; Della would be too wasted. Those phone calls had an adverse effect on me. I would be depressed for days.

The same problem arose when I invited Della to come to New York and spend some time with us. Della would get so excited. The three of us would plot and plan in great detail, discuss on the telephone all sorts of projects: shows and movies we would see, restaurants we would go to. And then, a day before Della was to arrive, she'd call and back out.

"Why? Why does she always do that?" I asked Mary.

"She's like you."

19

Today is Christmas Eve 1997. It's Della's birthday. She's thirty-five years old.

She has seven months to live.

When I called to wish her happy birthday, Della told me she had her dog walker take a snapshot of her with a throwaway camera she said she had bought expressly for her birthday picture. She told me she wanted a memento of her doggies and herself "on this memorable occasion." I asked her why this birthday was more memorable than any of the others and she said, "Because a bunch of times during the last year I truly didn't think I was going to make it to my thirty-fifth birthday."

I told her she was crazy.

She went on and on about the pictures. She told me she had the film developed at a one-hour photo store, but that the entire effort was a total waste of time and money. The reason: she looked so awful in the snapshots she ended up burning them.

She said, "It's funny there aren't many birthdays of mine I can remember. I do remember the one when I was sixteen and you gave me my gold Rolex watch. Well, you didn't exactly give it to me. You threw it at me while I was sitting in the back of a taxi. Remember that? It was my fault, I suppose. I provoked you that day. I did a lot of provoking in my life, if I do say so myself. Did you know my sweet sixteenth birthday was the last one I ever had with you, Daddy? With anybody, for that matter. Well, that's not really true. I had other birthdays with other people, but no more with you. I remember having one with my husband-for-a-month, Tony. Remember Tony? Remember how we got married on a Friday afternoon, December third, 1982, and divorced a month later on January third, 1983?

"As I recall, my birthday with Tony was memorable for its excruciating boredom. At least with you, Daddy, my birthdays were never dull. They weren't always fun. But if my birthdays weren't fun they were aggravating, and aggravating's better than boring. There must have been other birthdays with other people, but at the moment I don't remember them. My birthdays with you were fun. Did I just say that? You would always buy me a ton of presents. Too many, though I never complained. Sometimes the pile was as high as an elephant's eye. God, I'm wasted. Did I tell you I was writing a book entitled *Jesus Left the Building*? Yeah, I told you that too."

It was July 1998. And hot as hell. Della was working in her apartment trying to finish *Jesus Left the Building*. She telephoned me to say that her handwriting had changed drastically. No matter how slowly she wrote, the writing was wavy and lopsided and barely legible. She said she sat at her kitchen table and wrote and wrote and wrote to see if her handwriting would get any better. It didn't. She copied names and phone numbers into her address book wondering if she could read them. Often she couldn't.

"It must be my HIV medicine," she said.

Her beloved apartment had changed drastically too. Della had sold almost everything to pay for her drug habit, and Strickland's. She finally had to sell the last of her jewelry, the good stuff, the jewelry she liked the most. She sold some of her favorite paintings on the street. Her three all-time favorites she hung on her walls. That was the end of her paintings.

When everything she could hock was gone, Della was forced to go begging. Had I known, I would have been shocked. I paid most of her bills. Della was begging for drug money. She would sit on the pavement on the south side of Santa Monica Boulevard in Brentwood, across from the entrance to the small shopping mall where the California Pizza Kitchen is. She would hold out her favorite black suede peaked cap with a sign at her feet that read: PLEASE HELP ME. I AM STARVING AND HIV POSITIVE. Della would have sat at the entrance to the mall but was afraid I would see her; I often went there to have lunch with friends. I never knew my daughter was begging for money on the streets of Brentwood. As I said, had I known what Della was doing, I would have been shocked, mortified, and furious. Della said she was always worried friends of mine would see her and tell me. But no one ever did.

Sometimes, if she was up to it, Della would bring her beat-up guitar out to a street corner and sing Dylan songs. She loved to sing "Blowin' in the Wind." Della felt it was the story of her life. She'd make a few bucks singing Dylan songs, which Strickland would always grab for drugs.

Often, when Della went back to her apartment, Strickland would be there. For reasons known only to himself, Strickland would go nuts and start screaming at her. Della never knew why. Strickland would have the tip of his nose against the tip of Della's, his spit hitting her in the face, yelling, "You want the drugs as much as I do, don't you, you stupid bitch!"

Della would say yes.

"Then shut up!"

"But I didn't say anything."

Once in a while Strickland would raise his hand as if to strike Della and she'd flinch, but she said he never hit her. In fact, Della was often so stoned she really didn't know whether he hit her or not, but the next day there were never any bruises on Della's face or body. Sometimes Strickland would leave Della's apartment, shouting he was never going to see her again, slamming the door hard. It wasn't long after he'd gone that Della would telephone Strickland and beg him to come back.

During a hot Wednesday night in July, about a week after their last argument, Strickland and Della got into a huge fight. Bigger than most. Della had been drinking vodka. Strickland had just dusted a pint bottle of Maker's Mark bourbon and the two had done some freebasing. Della was screaming and yelling at Strickland. He was screaming and yelling at her. Neighbors told police they knocked on Della's walls repeatedly. They said what they heard coming out of her apartment was "pretty scary."

Della must have passed out. She didn't remember what happened next until she woke up at eight that morning to wave at Tom-the-dog-walker, and then at about eleven she woke for good. When she was *really* up and focused, and saw what she saw, the sight came very close to destroying her.

Maybe it eventually did.

Della telephoned Judy Ducharme, sobbing hysterically on the phone. She said, "Judy, something awful has happened. Something really terrible. It's like a nightmare, only it's true and I'm not dreaming."

Judy was alarmed. She could hear the panic in Della's voice. "What happened, Della?"

Judy said Della could barely talk. She kept starting and stopping and choking on her sobs. Finally she managed to say, "It's Strickland."

"What about him?"

"Please come over, Judy. Please. Right now!"

Judy Ducharme couldn't come over. Not that morning. Not the entire day. Judy told Della she wasn't feeling well. She said she thought she might have the flu. She was going to the doctor's that afternoon. It was an appointment she couldn't break. She had waited for the appointment for a week. Besides, Judy didn't want Della to catch whatever it was she had. "Like I say, I might have a flu bug, and you with your immune system as weak as it—"

Della hung up on her without saying good-bye.

Strickland had destroyed Della's apartment.

Whatever he could get his hands on of Della's had been smashed to smithereens, torn, or shredded. He tore up all of Della's clothes. He overturned all her tables. Everything that was on them lay shattered on the floor. He pulled Della's three favorite paintings from the walls and slashed them with his knife. He tore the air-conditioning unit from the window and threw it on the floor. Drawers were taken from her bureaus and smashed, the contents dumped all over the apartment. Then the drawers were thrown to the floor with such force they splintered and broke. Her bureau was pulled from the wall and thrown on top of the busted drawers.

Lamps were smashed, their metal stands bent, the wooden ones broken. Strickland must have used a heavy instrument, probably a hammer or the heels of his boots. Dishes were destroyed, the garbage bags was pulled out of the can under the sink, the garbage thrown all over the apartment. Milk was emptied onto the furniture, ketchup on the floors and walls. A jar of mustard was thrown against a wall, the jar smashed, the mustard everywhere. Clumps of mayonnaise were all over the place: on the floor, on the walls, on just about everything. Other items from the refrigerator—eggs, cream cheese, jars of jellies and jams—were tossed onto the kitchen and living room floors and tracked through the apartment. The fridge's shelves were pulled out and thrown around the kitchen. Strickland tried to rip the refrigerator's door off but couldn't. He left it open and dented from a kick. He stomped on the heads of the few dolls Della had left, smashing them to bits. The dolls Strickland destroyed were all dear to Della, and he knew it. She never pawned those dolls even when they really needed the money. He knew that too. That's probably why he destroyed every one of them.

Strickland squirted Della's paint on her rugs and threw paint on her walls. He broke the neck off her guitar, kicked in the body, and smashed her TV screen. He destroyed her video and DVD machines. Her shrine to me was obliterated. It simply didn't exist anymore. Strickland pulled Della's bookshelves from the walls and ripped apart as many paperbacks as he could. He smashed what was left of Della's valuable LP record collection. Everything Della owned was broken, busted, or ruined. Everything. It was a miracle Strickland didn't kill Della's three little dogs. They must have sat there and watched, terrified, poor things.

Other than her three dogs, Della's apartment was what mattered most to her. It was all she had. Her apartment was always neat and tidy to the point of obsession. Everything had its place, and now everything was destroyed, everything was gone. Strickland knew exactly how Della felt about her apartment, and short of killing her, he did what was most damaging to Della. Strickland knew if he did what he did, it would destroy her, and if that was his objective, he succeeded. Strickland might as well have committed murder.

I imagine Della spent the entire day sitting on the edge of her bed, too sick to go out, forced to stare at the devastation of her once cozy, neat little home that was now a disaster area. No television, no music, nothing. Her apartment, from the pictures Judy showed me days later, looked exactly like TV footage of the living rooms and bedrooms of homes destroyed by tornadoes. Della must have cried until she didn't have any tears left. She had to feel devastated, violated, and so very sad. Sad about her apartment, sad about Judy Ducharme not coming when she called, sad about me and her mother living miles and miles away in New York and London, enjoying ourselves to the hilt, doing whatever it was we were doing, not giving a damn about Della. Did anybody care if Della was happy or sad? Apparently not. I'm convinced, at that moment in time, Della believed absolutely no one was thinking about her. I'd bet on that.

Under a pile of debris, Della found a bottle of vodka. It

hadn't been smashed and was almost full. She also found the cocaine she had hidden from Strickland under the floorboard in her closet. Della cleared the debris off her daybed, and she and her little dogs lay down. Della propped some pillows behind her head and stretched out. The dogs lay at her feet. It was roughly four thirty on a Thursday afternoon.

What am I going to do now? she thought. *I could never look at Strickland again, and I don't ever expect him to come back. What am I going to use for money?* She had none, and nothing at all to hock. *What am I going to do for food? How am I going to feed my doggies? Am I ever going to get better? Probably not.*

Della began snorting the cocaine from the top of a book she'd been reading, and drinking the vodka, wondering . . .

Maybe, she thought, *this is rock bottom.*

20

Mary had telephoned Della earlier in the week and told her our plans. We would be arriving on Friday afternoon, and the two of us were looking forward to spending the rest of Friday and all of Saturday and Sunday being slugs with Della, soaking up the sun on the Peninsula roof garden, going to some fancy restaurants. If the weather wasn't great Friday, Saturday, or Sunday, we'd all go to the movies. It would be the first movie with Della since I'd almost gotten into the fight with the guy sitting on the other side of her. I was skeptical. Mary said we could take the chance. If there was trouble, she would handle it.

I had made an appointment for Della on the following Monday afternoon with an HIV specialist at UCLA Medical Center. We intended to take Della to the appointment, then Mary and I would fly back to New York first thing Tuesday morning.

Mary and I had been getting along terrifically over the last few months and were talking about getting married. Della was

ecstatic about the whole idea. So was I. I remember being in
an exceptionally good mood on the plane ride from New York
to Los Angeles. I teased the stewardesses and had a generally
fine time. Mary was doing her best to ignore my carrying on.
She tried to concentrate on her book. She hadn't decided yet
whether it was a good or bad thing when I was in an *exceptionally* good mood.

We took a limousine from the airport to the Peninsula. I always took a limousine from the airport and always used the
same driver, Danny Cahill. Danny had been driving me since he
started his limousine service "a hundred years ago," as he liked
to say. I used Danny's car phone to call some friends, say hello,
and tell them we hoped to see them, but it was all contingent on
how Della felt.

When we arrived at the Peninsula, there was a message waiting for me from my secretary. "What the hell could be *that* important?" I asked Mary.

I telephoned Loretta from the hotel's reception desk.

"Call Della's mother," she told me. "It's urgent." I knew it
had to be something about Della. Our daughter's predicaments
were the only reason her mother and I talked.

I called the number my secretary gave me in London. When
Della's mother answered, I said, "What is it *this* time?"

She said, "Della's dead."

When I finished talking to Della's mother, I laid the mobile
phone down on the counter of the Peninsula's reception desk
and walked outside. I reached into my pocket and took out
a snow globe I had brought for my daughter. Inside was the

Empire State Building. On top of the tiny building was a tiny sign that read NEW YORK CITY. I bought the snow globe for Della at Kennedy Airport, the first one I'd purchased for her in a long time.

I took a path that wound its way alongside the hotel. I walked until I was alone; no hotel employees walking by, no guests, no one. Then I threw the snow globe with all my might against a stone wall. It smashed into tiny bits and pieces.

The next day, Saturday, I received a message at the hotel from Della's mother. The message said, "Della's will states that she wishes to be cremated. She wants her ashes taken out to sea and scattered by the wind in the Pacific Ocean. Also her will states that Della has left everything to me."

I thought the message was strange. Della had never mentioned anything about a will, wanting to be cremated, or having her ashes scattered in the Pacific Ocean. Why would she, as sick as she was, go to all the trouble of seeing a lawyer and having an involved legal document drawn up?

I would have tried to talk Della out of being cremated. To me being cremated meant emptying something like an ashtray full of cigar ashes and having the ashes scattered by the wind in the Pacific Ocean. But what did I know? Della could very well have wanted to be cremated and might have spoken to her mother about it. Particularly since she was in such bad health. And as far as leaving everything to her mother, how much was there to leave? And why not? Della loved her mother.

I had my secretary call Della's mother and tell her I wanted to see my daughter once before she was cremated. Della's mother granted me my request but told my secretary to pass along a message to me to do it quickly. Loretta told me Della's mother was flying to Los Angeles from London as soon as she could get a reservation. She wanted to get on with the cremation arrangements the minute she arrived. She made it known that my visit to the mortuary should be over and done with before she set foot in California. Somewhere in my dense fog of grief I wondered where it was written that Della's mother had been appointed commander-in-chief of *our* daughter's funeral arrangements.

I told Mary, "If that's the way she wants it, fine. I'm too screwed up, too depressed, and too tired to argue with her."

21

Later that day, I asked Judy Ducharme if she wanted to go with me to the mortuary to have a last look at Della. Judy said she did. Mary didn't go with us. She thought Judy and I should be by ourselves with Della.

The problem was Judy. She was a mess; she couldn't stop crying. When I picked her up at her house to take her to the funeral home she was sobbing and barely able to catch her breath. She cried during the entire ride to the mortuary and kept repeating, "It was the only time. She *really* needed me. It was the only time. The only time it happened."

"The only time what happened?" I asked.

"The only time in my entire life I let Della down. She needed me the night she telephoned. But I couldn't go. I was sick. It was the only time it happened."

I tried my best to console Judy, but nothing seemed to work. She just continued sobbing and babbling. "In the Malibu school they gave . . . they gave out gold stars . . . for doing excellent homework. I helped Della with her homework . . . and when . . . and when she got her first gold star, she was so excited. She told the . . . the . . . the teacher I helped her. And then . . . and then later . . . later she got another gold star and the teacher and . . . and the teacher said, 'I'll bet you got this star because Judy helped you with your homework.'" Judy sobbed between gulps of air. "Della was very creative," Judy said. "Della decorated our entire bedroom in Malibu with . . . with pretty pictures she cut out from . . . from magazines and pasted them on the walls. You had a fit when you saw it and . . . and . . . and had to repaint the entire room. You may . . . may have punished Della but . . . but Della was very creative."

Judy sat beside me in my automobile, mumbling Della stories and sobbing, for the entire ride. When we arrived at the mortuary, Judy and I walked inside holding hands. In my free hand I held a box of Kleenex. I gave Judy the box, sat her down, and told her to wait in the lobby.

"Judy, you're completely distraught. I don't think you should see Della in your present state. You might collapse when you see her."

Judy agreed not to see Della.

I told the attendant it would be just me viewing my daughter. The attendant started saying something about not having enough time to prepare Della's body properly. "We're sorry about that. You see the problem was, we're awfully backed up and—"

"I don't give a damn what your problem was or is, or anything," I snapped. "Just bring me my daughter, *now*!"

The attendant nodded and led me to a viewing room. I took

a seat in an old high-backed leather armchair. I sat in that chair for ten minutes staring at my sneakers. Then the room's doors opened and another attendant rolled in a gurney.

Della was lying on top of the gurney, covered up to her neck with a white sheet.

She looked horrible.

So this was going to be my last memory of my once-pretty blond-haired daughter? I stood up, moved to another old high-backed leather armchair, and carried the chair as far away from the gurney as I could get. Sometimes I stared at the gurney from where I sat, my hands clasped between my legs. Most of the time I looked straight ahead or down at the floor. I finally got up the nerve to walk over to Della.

I stood next to the gurney looking down at my daughter. I thought, *Della's thirty-six, but she could easily pass for a woman of fifty-six.* I returned to the chair that was as far away from the gurney as I could move it. I sat there staring at my clasped hands. I stayed in that position, looking at my hands, for a long time. I wondered why Della's mother was preventing Judy Ducharme and me from going to Della's apartment. I thought a long time about my ex-wife's bewildering orders. The most bewildering of which was that *nothing* of Della's was to be given to me and Judy.

But Della's mother's orders were too late to stop Judy Ducharme. She had gone to Della's apartment the previous day as soon as the police had left, and before Della's mother could order the lock to be changed. Judy took photographs of the wrecked apartment. She held on to those photographs and eventually gave them to me when enough time had passed. She knew better than to let me see the pictures that day. She was smart.

Judy even gathered up some mementos of Della's: her favorite black suede cap, pictures of the two of us, a little chain with two charms Mary had given her that Della wore around her neck. The charms read Mind and Body. Judy found the practically unreadable pages that Della called her diary, an almost empty address-appointment book, and lots of letters. She gave them all to me. But Judy couldn't find any of Della's writing.

I couldn't change anything now. It was too late. What was done was done, and there was no looking back. But I kept looking back. I couldn't help myself. When, I wondered, do I put on my hair shirt? When do I begin beating my chest, making my *mea culpa*s? And who the hell am I making *mea culpa*s for? Della or myself?

22

I sat there, growing more and more uncomfortable in that smelly mortuary viewing room, staring at my hands, tormented by the litany of my mistakes. I wasn't thinking of Della and the good times we had together. Just the bad scenes.

I thought of when I walked out of my marriage and my home, how a terrified Della grabbed my leg and how, when I tried pulling my leg away, my heel smacked her jaw. I couldn't possibly have comprehended how truly miserable Della was that morning at our Hollywood house.

Or when Della came to my office to tell me she was leaving home and I simply let her go, never showing any kindness or consideration, not expressing to my daughter the least bit of love, just giving her money, telling her to go, and feeling relief, which Della must have heard in my voice. If only I had insisted she stay, she might still be alive. If only I'd had the patience and wisdom that morning I have today.

Or the afternoon I allowed the girlfriend I was living with at the time to talk me into packing up all of Della's prize possessions from her room in the little upside-down house on St. Ives Drive and sending them to storage so the room could become a guest room. I tried to guess how Della felt that morning, having just suffered my throwing her out of our home, then out of her room. What must she have thought when she saw all her belongings gone? Fortunately for me I would never be able to understand fully the misery Della felt that day, how abandoned and lonely and scared she was at that moment of her life.

When would I ever stop recalling those memories? Never, I suppose.

But then what do you do with a child who will not listen to you? I tried to give Della everything, but it didn't matter. Nothing mattered to her.

Sitting in the old high-backed leather armchair, in the seedy mortuary viewing room, I agonized over those horrendous memories. I became convinced I had killed my daughter. It wasn't an overdose. It wasn't suicide. It wasn't Strickland. It was me.

I moaned out loud and began to weep quietly. I wasn't crying for Della; I was crying for myself. I was crying for all my regrets, for all the horrible decisions I made concerning my baby daughter, the little girl who took her first steps into my arms and was now lying dead from drugs and alcohol on a mortuary gurney just twenty feet away. Then, holding my head in my hands and rocking my body back and forth in the old armchair, I suddenly shouted, in a strange high-pitched voice, "Tough love doesn't work!"

An attendant opened the door and looked into the room.

"Are you okay?" she asked.

I nodded, never taking my head out of my hands, never stopping my rocking, or weeping, or staring at the floor. The attendant stepped back into the hall and quietly shut the door. Then, continuing to talk to myself, I said, "I *still* don't have any answers. I *still* don't know how to be a father to a child hooked on drugs. What was I to do? All my experience taught me nothing. I tried everything and nothing worked. I practically forced Della to go to a rehab place but she refused. I tried tricking her and that didn't work. How do you make a teenager do something she doesn't want to do? There aren't any answers to that question. If there are, I sure as hell don't know them."

I stopped talking to myself and just rocked my body back and forth in that stupid armchair. I sat there and cried for a long time. I was shattered. Eventually I stood, turned, looked at Della one last time, and walked out of the room.

In the lobby of the mortuary I saw Judy Ducharme sitting on a chair. She wasn't crying anymore. But now I couldn't stop. Judy stood and took me in her arms.

She said, "You did everything you could for Della. You gave her *everything*."

But enough love, I thought.

I put my head on Judy's shoulder. I stayed there for a few minutes. Then I stopped crying, pulled my head back, and stood up straight. Judy hooked her arm in mine, and the two of us walked out of the funeral home.

23

Outside the sun was shining. There was a light Santa Ana wind. I told Judy the warm breeze felt good. While the two of us walked to my car, I wondered if I would ever feel good about myself again.

The one thing I wanted most and never found were pages from Della's book, *Jesus Left the Building*. I wanted to read her book, or parts of it, or pages of it at least. Since Judy Ducharme couldn't find any writing, I was sure the book had not survived Strickland's devastating temper tantrum.

Maybe given half a break, and some help from me or somebody else, Della could have been a famous writer or painter. Who knows?

I wondered, the day Della died, if she thought about me, about her mother, about her three dogs before she overdosed?

"No," said my mother. "Suicidal people don't think about things like their parents or who will take care of their dogs when they kill themselves. Suicides don't give a damn about those things. Della was too inconsiderate to think about anything but herself."

Imagine, my mother told me that just hours after Della died.

I can tell you this: Della didn't want to die. She wanted to continue waking up in the morning and playing with her three little doggies. She wanted to smell the tops of their little heads. She wanted to feel their fur and warm stomachs again. She wanted to bundle up when it was cold out, smell fresh spring air. She wanted to go with me to a Kings hockey game as long as they were playing an eastern team like Boston or Philly or Montreal.

Della wanted to stay alive to see if someone would publish her book. She wanted Judy to take care of her when she grew old. She wanted to paint again. Maybe in time her paintings would not have been so morose. She wanted to see the leaves change colors in the fall. She wanted to eat a hot dog with mustard on a fresh hot dog roll.

Della wanted to hug Weezy. She wanted to see the old gang from the *Gong Show* studio days, talk to Marge Reck, and Jennifer Cobb, get a hug from Gene Gene the Dancing Machine again and Jaye P. Morgan. Della loved Gene and Jaye P.

She wanted to kiss me in the morning and smell the Lilac Vegetal shaving lotion on my cheek. She wanted to continue to see Mary. She wanted to be part of our wedding procession when Mary and I were married. Maybe Mary would have made her a bridesmaid or her maid of honor. I know our wedding was one affair Della wanted to attend in the worst way.

I'm also sure Della wanted to see her mother again, and squeeze her, and smell her, and tell her she was a good mother.

And who knows, maybe in Della's lifetime scientists would find a cure for HIV/AIDS, and Della would regain her health. I'm absolutely sure she wanted to be around for that possibility.

I know Della made a stupid mistake. Snorting as much cocaine as she did and drinking all that vodka was just plain stupid. And she was bound to make a stupid mistake, being the druggie she was. But I'm as sure as I can be that Della did not commit suicide.

Millions of children take drugs at one time or another and survive to live normal lives and become great successes. A small percentage don't. My experience tells me that parents should try as hard as they can to keep their children away from drugs. I know from my experiences with my daughter that it was hard for me, and her mother, and for those who loved my daughter.

Imagine how hard it was for Della.

They say we're alive until the last person who knew us dies.

In that case, Della Charlotte Barris still lives.

DELLA CHARLOTTE BARRIS
1962–1998

ACKNOWLEDGMENTS

I would like to thank Will Balliett, Judy Ducharme, and the late Loretta Strickland for their help. I would also like to thank my agent Jennifer Lyons, Danny Endy, Dick Clark, Cathie Pelletier, and Betsy Nolan for their encouragement, and Mary Barris for imparting her perseverance to me; and my editor, Sarah Hochman, for her support and her incredible contributions to this book.

About the Author

Chuck Barris is a former television show creator and producer, whose credits include *The Dating Game, The Newlywed Game, The Gong Show,* and *Treasure Hunt.* He is the author of several books, including *Who Killed Art Deco?, The Big Question, Confessions of a Dangerous Mind* (adapted into a major motion picture), and *You and Me, Babe: A Novel.* Barris and his wife, Mary, live in Manhattan.